Landscape Structures & Decks

Handyman Club Library™
Handyman Club of America
Minneapolis, Minnesota

Landscape Structures & Decks

CREDITS

Mike Vail
Vice President, Products & Business Development

Tom Carpenter
Director of Books & New Media Development

Mark Johanson
Book Products Development Manager

Dan Cary
Photo Production Coordinator

Chris Marshall
Editorial Coordinator

Jim Barrett
Writer

Mark Johanson, Chris Marshall
Contributing Writers

Bill Nelson
Series Design, Art Direction and Production

Mark Macemon
Lead Photographer

Kim Bailey, Ralph Karlen
Photography

John Nadeau
Technical Advisor and Builder

Troy Johnson
Builder

Craig Claeys
Contributing Illustrator

Dan Kennedy
Book Production Manager

PHOTO CREDITS

Pages 6, 7
Hedberg Aggregates
Pages 9, 11, 55, 73, 74, 75, 76, 93, 94
Southern Pine Council
Pages 9, 17
Portland Cement Association
Pages 8, 10, 55
Keystone Retaining Wall Systems
Page 17
Brick Institute of America
Pages 7, 8, 10, 11, 73, 74, 94, 95, 147, 148
California Redwood Association
Pages 6, 7, 11, 41, 49, 50, 51, 52
Lilypons Water Gardens
Pages 9, 74
Jim Barrett

Special Thanks To
Sara & Kirk Jensen, Kevin Jesser

ISBN 1-58159-008-3

Handyman Club of America
12301 Whitewater Drive
Minnetonka, Minnesota 55343

Table of Contents

Landscape Structures & Decks

Introduction 5
Ideas for Landscape
Structures & Decks 6

Building Landscape
Structures 12
Landscape Building Basics 13
Patios & Walkways 16
• Interlocking Pavers 18
• Flagstone 30
• Loose Fill 36

Water Gardens 40
• Flexible Liner Ponds 42
• Filters, Fountains & Falls. 49
• Stocking Your Water Garden 52

Wall Structures 54
• Interlocking Block. 58
• Landscape Timbers 65

Fences & Gates. 72
• Stick-built Fences 79
• Gates 86
• Prefabricated Fence Panels 88

Building Decks. 90
Deck Basics 96
Deckbuilding: An Overview. . . . 106
Deck Layout 108
Footings 113
Ledgers. 118
Framing 122
Decking 134
Stairs 138
Railings & Accessories 146
Finishing. 156

INDEX 158

Introduction

For any homeowner, the backyard provides unique opportunities for recreation and relaxation. But for the handyman, outdoor space provides another important benefit: it is a place to design, to build and to put your skills and creativity on display.

Unlike your house, your yard is a very forgiving canvas for building projects: holes can be filled in; grass and small plants will grow back; and just about any structure can be easily removed and replaced with something you like better. For these reasons, many handymen and weekend remodelers especially enjoy working outdoors.

Although many backyard building projects involve more muscle than talent, it helps to know exactly what you need to do before you strip off the sod for your new patio or set the posts for your new deck. In this book, produced by the Handyman Club of America for the exclusive use of our members, you'll find all the information you need to undertake today's most popular backyard building projects. In fact, *Landscape Structures & Decks* was planned and produced to focus solely on the building projects the members of our club are most interested in accomplishing.

The first section of this book is devoted to landscape construction projects: building patios, walkways, walls, fences, gates and garden ponds. Quite a number of building materials are used to make these structures, from cast concrete pavers to natural stone; from prefabricated fence panels to raw exterior lumber. For each project, you'll find a wealth of helpful information, along with beautiful full-color photographs that take you through each major step of the process. It's like watching a landscape contractor from start to finish as he completes a job—but without leaving the comfort of your favorite chair.

The second section of this book focuses on a backyard building project that's on just about every handyman's wish list or resume: building a deck. In these pages, you'll find all the basic information you need to build a simple deck, but much more. Because most of us know enough about basic carpentry to design and build a basic square deck that has all the charm of a wooden pallet, our deck section aims a little higher. In it you'll see every detail and every painstaking step

as we create a glorious, two-tier feature deck that quickly became the envy of the entire neighborhood where it was built. How-to instructions for the planning and layout, pouring foundation piers, building the undercarriage, laying the deck boards, and dressing out the deck with stairs, railings, fascia and even benches are all shown in exciting full-color detail. By the time you've finished reviewing this section, you'll have most of the knowledge and skills you need to build a unique deck that's the envy of *your* neighborhood.

Think ahead to your next backyard barbecue or party. Now imagine it taking place on your brand new paver patio or your spacious new deck. Remember slogging through the mud last summer to weed your garden or pick your tomatoes? Now imagine making the trek on a neat walkway made of natural stones, and perhaps stopping along the way to gaze into your new garden pond. There is almost no end to the satisfaction and payback you can obtain from even the simplest backyard building or landscaping project.

Ideas for Landscape Structures & Decks

On the following pages you'll find examples of a number of deck-building and landscape construction projects. They range from casual and simple to elaborate. In addition, each of the major sections of this book has a shorter gallery of completed projects to help spur your imagination when designing your own backyard building effort. While we did our best to choose a wide range of projects to help with your initial planning, you'll probably want to extend your search for inspiration beyond the pages of this book. You can visit your local library or bookstore and thumb through other printed material, or consult with designers or landscape architects for their thoughts. But perhaps the best way to generate ideas you know will work out well is simply to walk through your own neighborhood and take note of what your neighbors have done, looking for successes as well as projects that, for any number of reasons, didn't pan out.

A raised flower bed created with interlocking blocks cast from concrete provides a nice contrast to the warm wood deck tones in this emerging suburban neighborhood.

A figure-eight shaped garden pond and a planting bed add interest to an otherwise flat and ordinary lawn. The symmetrical shapes of these two structures introduce elements of nature to the backyard, while preserving the neatly clipped appearance favored by this homeowner.

Cobblestones and poured concrete join forces to create these elegant backyard steps—and complement the interlocking block retaining wall.

Exotic foliage thrives in this flexible-liner water garden, adding a taste of the tropics to a Midwestern backyard.

Interesting angles and well-placed railings allow this low-level deck to blend in perfectly in this rustic backyard setting. A little creativity and vision result in an original deck that picks up and keeps on going where rectangles and simple "L's" leave off.

RIGHT: A sturdy arbor-and-trellis creates a canopy of climbing plants and beautiful blossoms above a custom-built fence and gate.

BELOW: The austere brick facade of this contemporary house is softened by a gently meandering planting bed built with interlocking concrete blocks.

BOTTOM: Swimmers step down to the pool in style as they enjoy the graceful lines and easy access created by a well-designed deck.

Charm and grace are the two qualities that come to mind when passing by this lovely picket fence.

This floating deck proves that a good design is at home anywhere in your yard.

Tumbled pavers have the look and feel of an authentic cobblestone street in this spacious patio.

ABOVE: An urban retreat is established in a big-city backyard through the use of an efficient deck, a slatted privacy fence and some cleverly arranged potted plants.

RIGHT: A multi-media showcase can be put on display by carefully combining several backyard building materials, as these steps and adjoining wall demonstrate.

Garden ponds don't need to look artificial. Surrounding this flexible-liner pond with prairie grasses and natural flagstone lends an untamed feeling to the paver walkway and cast-paver coping stones that border most of the pond.

The feel of a Japanese garden is created more by the landscape structures than the plantings in this well-designed setting.

Natural stone, greenery and weathered wood are combined for an inviting effect in this lovely garden sanctuary.

Building Landscape Structures

Landscape Building Basics

Building landscape structures is not an exact science, as some forms of interior carpentry and woodworking are. The common step shared by most projects is quite simple: moving dirt. And even though there are do's and don't's related to digging, the basic ingredients are a sturdy shovel, a strong back, a wheelbarrow or garden cart, and a spot to dispose of any earth you remove from the project area.

Beyond digging, most landscape building projects also require you to do some sort of ground preparation: leveling off an excavation site, filling in low spots, and tamping down loose soil. Then a subbase, most often made from compactible gravel, is laid and tamped for most projects (exceptions being garden ponds and informal loose-fill walkways or patios laid over stable soil with good drainage). Landscape fabric should be layered into most landscape building projects to control weed growth and keep subbase or base materials from settling together.

Once the subbase is created, the individual projects diverge quickly into the unique steps they require.

Digging tools are required for just about any landscape construction project. A basic set includes: (A) a hoe for moving loose soil and mixing concrete; (B) a general-purpose spade; (C) a hand tamper; (D) a posthole digger; and (E) a wheelbarrow.

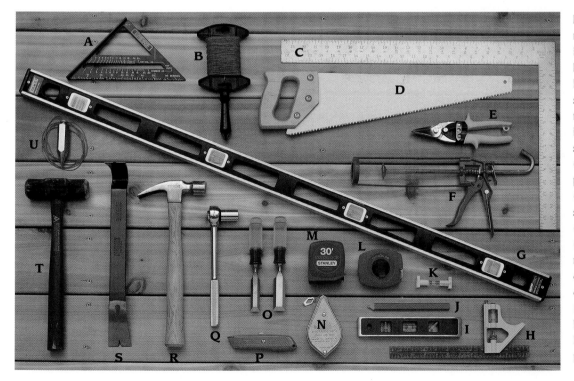

Hand tools are used in most landscape building projects, if only for layout and leveling. A basic set includes: (A) speed square; (B) mason's line; (C) framing square; (D) hand saw; (E) aviator snips; (F) caulk gun; (G) carpenter's level (4 ft.); (H) combination square; (I) spirit level; (J) pencil; (K) line level; (L) 50 ft. roll tape; (M) rigid tape measure; (N) chalkline; (O) wood chisels; (P) utility knife; (Q) socket wrench; (R) hammer; (S) flat pry bar; (T) hand maul; (U) plumb bob.

Coarse sand is used as a base material for setting pavers and natural stones, and as a base for flexible pond liners. Fine sand can also be purchased at most landscape materials centers, but it has little application in landscape construction.

Decorative rock, like the pink quartz above, is used in loose-fill walkways and patios, planting beds and as a border treatment. Styles vary by region. It is relatively expensive.

Compactible gravel is used as a subbase material in most landscape construction projects. Known in some regions as "Class V" or "Class II" (lower numbers denote smaller aggregate), it improves drainage and can be tamped to create a stable base.

Pea gravel is also used mostly as a drainage material but can be used successfully as a border treatment around plantings. It is not recommended for use as a loose fill for walkways or patios.

Trap rock is a slate-based aggregate used mostly to create dry wells and to provide drainage. It can be used for decorative purposes in some situations. It is not compactible.

River rock is used mostly as a drainage material when backfilling, as with a retaining wall. It can also be used for decorative or loose-fill purposes. It is sold according to the diameter of the stones (⅜ in., ¾ in., and 1½ in. are typical). As a general rule, use larger diameter stones for walkways and patios, and smaller diameter (or a combination of smaller and larger) for drainage fill. 1½ in. dia. river rock is shown above.

MATERIALS FOR LANDSCAPE CONSTRUCTION

Landscape fabric is a weather-resistant, semiporous fabric that inhibits weed growth, but allows water to pass through. It is frequently installed between layers of subbase and base material to keep the upper layer from settling down into the lower layer.

Landscape edging has several purposes in landscape construction. It is laid around planting beds to keep plantings segregated from the lawn. It is installed around patios and walkways to contain subbase and base materials. And it can be used as a decorative treatment to create visible barriers around landscape elements. Better quality edging is more rigid.

Rules for Building Outdoors

❑ *WATCH OUT FOR BURIED LINES. Always contact your local public utilities to identify the location of buried power lines and gas lines before you dig.Utilities will provide line location identification as a free service.*

❑ *RESEARCH BUILDING CODES. Although building permits may not be required for many landscape projects, most municipalities enforce outdoor building restrictions. Allowable height of fences and walls, and minimum distance from city land and other property lines are two common areas subject to restrictions.*

❑ *DISCUSS PLANS WITH YOUR NEIGHBORS. Your outdoor building project will likely be within the field of vision of your neighbors. As a courtesy, share plans with neighbors and give them the chance to raise objections or concerns before you start working. As a rule, maintain a setback of at least 1 ft. from property lines.*

❑ *BE AWARE OF WEATHER CONDITIONS. Working outdoors can be highly strenuous, especially on hot, humid days. Avoid working in direct sunlight, drink plenty of water, and wear light-colored clothing (long pants and a long-sleeve shirt for protection). Work with a partner when possible. Don't work in threatening weather.*

❑ *TAKE CARE OF POWER CORDS. Extension cords are a danger and a nuisance. Keep them out of traffic areas. Always use exterior-rated extension cords with ground-fault circuit interruption (GFCI) protection.*

RENTAL TOOLS FOR LANDSCAPE CONSTRUCTION

Sod kicker   Gas-powered auger   Plate vibrator (power tamper)

A sod kicker is a hand-powered blade that removes sod in usable strips that can be laid elsewhere in your yard. **A gas-powered auger** makes quick work of digging holes for fence posts or deck footings. Most require two people to operate. **A plate vibrator** (also called a power tamper or a jumping jack) provides greater compaction of subbase material than a hand tamper, with greater uniformity and less effort.

Patios & Walkways

Patios and walkways are the most prominent features in typical outdoor living spaces. They can be built in just about any size or shape with a wide range of building material options. Pavers and natural stone are the most popular materials for patios and walkways today because they're relatively easy to install and they can conform to the sizes and shapes that best fit in with your landscape design.

You can also build walkways and patios by creating a stable base, bordering it with landscape edging, and covering the area with loose fill, such as aggregate, mulch or bark. Loose-fill projects are the simplest to build but are limited mostly to more informal or rustic environments. Traditionally, patios and walkways have also been built with poured concrete. In some situations, poured concrete is a good landscape option, but working with it involves a multitude of specific masonry skills that are not shown in this book. If you'd like to install a poured concrete feature, you can find information at libraries and bookstores, and in other volumes of the *Handyman Club Library.*

While precast concrete or brick pavers are sold in a vast assortment of shapes, sizes and colors (See pages 20 to 21), resourceful do-it-yourselfers sometimes prefer to cast their own concrete pavers in original shapes and sizes, using dry premixed concrete. To make your own pavers, simply construct a form from plywood or hardboard and fill it with concrete mixture (if you live in a colder climate, making pavers is a great winter project to prepare yourself for the spring building season). Another way to achieve the look of pavers or even natural stone is to stamp patterns into freshly poured concrete. Most concrete suppliers sell stamping tools that can impart the look of flagstone or pavers into the concrete.

The main challenges when building patios and walkways are choosing a design and materials that blend with your home and yard, then doing careful installation work to create a stable, weed-free subbase and a pleasing arrangement of the building materials.

Brick pavers are fired from natural clay and feature color variations that add to their decorative appeal. On larger surfaces they can be formed into nonsquare shapes with only minimal cutting.

Loose-fill walkways and patios are simple to create and have a natural appearance that blends in well in rustic or casual settings.

Stamped concrete gives the general appearance of pavers or natural stone, but at a fraction of the cost. The paver shapes and textures are stamped in with a stamping tool as soon as the fresh concrete has set up.

Cast your own pavers from concrete for unique walkways and patios. The lizard-shaped, custom-cast pavers above form interesting patterns when interlocked.

Flagstones are used to build very traditional patios and walkways that can fit in well in either a casual or a formal setting. The joints between stones usually are filled with a mixture of sand and mortar or cement to keep the stones in place.

Interlocking Pavers

Interlocking pavers have become an extremely popular surfacing material for patios, walks and driveways. They're relatively easy to install and, when set on a firm, properly prepared subbase, they'll hold up to foot traffic and heavy loads under a variety of weather conditions, without sinking, cracking, or shifting.

Set in sand, the pavers "flex" with changing temperatures, soil saturation levels, conditions and loads, rather than cracking as poured concrete patios some-

times will. Because of their high compressive strength, interlocking pavers are used for many commercial applications, such as public sidewalks and crosswalks, outdoor shopping malls, and even industrial equipment yards. Another advantage to building with sand-set interlocking pavers is that the individual units are easy to replace or reset, should the need arise.

About pavers

The two basic categories of pavers are brick pavers and concrete pavers. Brick pavers are fired in kilns from clay, and concrete pavers are cast in forms. Brick pavers tend to have more natural warmth and less of a hard, symmetrical appearance than concrete pavers, but they're more expensive. Concrete pavers are denser and generally available in a much wider range of sizes and shapes and are more common today.

Planning a paver patio or walkway

Plan the finished patio or walkway dimensions to avoid excess cutting of pavers. If you have the pavers on hand, lay out two rows on a flat surface (such as a driveway) to represent the width and length of the patio, providing the desired spacing between each unit. Take into account the width of any border pavers and

Anatomy of a Concrete Paver Structure

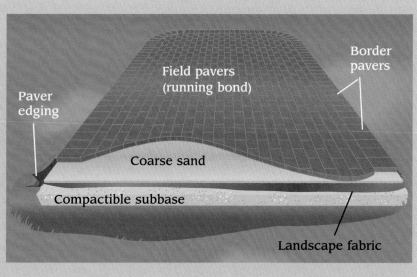

An interlocking paver patio or walkway consists of several different building materials layered together into the excavation area. After removing the sod and topsoil in the work area, a layer of compactible gravel is laid and tamped to 4 in. thick. Then, special paver edging is installed around the border of the project area. Landscape fabric is laid over the compactible gravel, a 1 in. layer of coarse sand is poured and leveled on top of the landscape fabric. The pavers are laid in pattern, starting at one corner, then filling in throughout the field area. Finally, a mixture of sand and mortar or Portland cement is swept into the gaps between pavers. When moistened with water, the mixture hardens to hold the pavers in place.

edging materials. Most concrete pavers have nubs on the sides that provide uniform $1/16$ or $1/8$ in. gaps that are filled with dry sand or a mixture of sand and mortar on Portland cement to lock the pavers in place. See the *Tip* on page 21 for information on estimating the number of pavers your project will require.

If building a patio that will adjoin your house, use the door threshold, stoop, or steps/stairs as your initial guideline for determining the final height and slope for your patio. Ideally, the transitional step-up from the patio surface to the door threshold or first step tread should be between 5 and $7\frac{1}{2}$ in. You'll also need to plan for a slight slope (typically $1/8$ in. per foot) when laying out your project. The slope should direct water runoff away from your house. In addition, a slight crown in the overall surface from side to side will help facilitate water runoff on both patios and walkways.

TOOLS FOR SETTING PAVERS

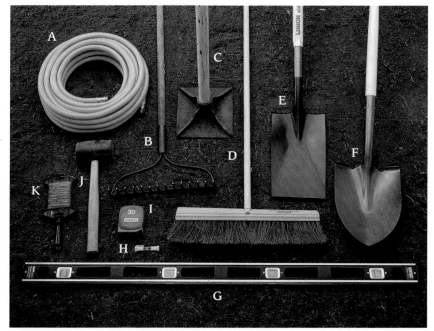

Tools for installing paver patios and walkways include: (A) a garden hose; (B) a garden rake; (C) a hand tamper; (D) a stiff-bristled push broom; (E) a square-nose spade; (F) a standard spade; (G) a carpenter's level; (H) a line level; (I) a tape measure; (J) a rubber mallet; and (K) a mason's line.

LAYOUT PATTERNS FOR RECTANGLE PAVERS

Running Bond

Standard Basketweave

Herringbone

Offset Basketweave

Running Stack

Two-to-one Basketweave

OPTIONAL PAVER SHAPES & PATTERNS

Offset diamond shapes can be combined into dozens of pattern variations, especially when combined with square pavers. An X-shaped repeating medallion pattern is indicated above, and a running diamond pattern below.

Split octagon with offset square ends can be combined to form any of the most common patterns. Note that the pavers are arranged in mirror-image pairs.

Cobblestones are noninterlocking square or rectangular pavers, typically antiqued using a tumbling process. The roundovers at the edges of the top surfaces create a quilted look when installed in groups.

Zig-zag shapes have a larger amount of interlocking surface area, and are best used in running bond types of patterns.

Estimating Paver Quantities

To estimate how many pavers you need to complete your project, the most accurate method is to arrange a handful of the pavers you'll be using into a small section of the pattern, then measure the total length and width of the section. Divide the measurements by the number of pavers it contains for an average per-unit length and width that allow for the gaps between pavers. Divide the planned width and length of the patio or walkway by the average unit dimensions and add 10% to the total for waste.

Paver patios

If the patio you plan to build will adjoin a house, use a door threshold or steps to determine the height of the patio closest to the house. Ideally, the transitional step up from the patio surface to the door threshold or first step tread should be between 5 and 7½ in. Patio surfaces should slope away from the building so that water drains away from the foundation, so the patio side closest to the house is the "high" side. You must establish and maintain a drainage slope across the patio surface from high side to low side as you build your patio.

Installing a paver patio

1 For square or rectangular patios, outline the patio area with wood stakes and mason's line **(See FIGURE A).** Attach the lines roughly 4 in. above ground level. Position the stakes about 2 ft. outside the planned patio area. Check the layout for square by measuring diagonally from corner to corner; the layout is square when the diagonals are equal.

2 Use a line level to level the mason's line on what will be the patio's high side first. Once the string is level, mark its height on the stake at either end **(See FIGURE B).** You'll be using this high side as a starting point and adjusting the remaining three string lines to it.

3 Use a carpenter's level to transfer level marks from the leveled string to an adjacent stake at one corner **(See FIGURE C).** Adjust the second string line to this mark, level the string with a line level, then mark the stake at the opposite end. Repeat this procedure at each corner until all strings are level with each other. The strings should barely touch one another where they intersect.

4 The patio should slope gradually so water drains away from buildings or follows the natural drainage pattern of your yard. The slope should be ⅛ in. per ft. At each low-end stake, measure and mark the amount of drop from the level mark and retie the strings at these marks **(See FIGURE D).** Adjust the intersecting

FIGURE A: Drive two stakes approximately 2 ft. outside each of the prospective four corners of the patio area. Attach mason's line between the stakes to mark the length and width of the patio. The points where the strings intersect between the stakes determines the actual corners of the patio.

FIGURE B: Level the mason's line on the high side of the layout using a line level. Mark its height on the stakes at each end. This level line serves as a reference to level the other three layout string lines.

string at the low end to this height. Leave the strings in place to serve as guides for excavating the patio area.

5 Clear the layout area of all plantings, large stones and other obstructions. If you're installing the patio in a grass yard, remove all sod within the patio area and 6 to 8 in. beyond the strings on each side **(See FIGURE E).** Save some of the sod for filling in any bare spots around the patio after it's installed.

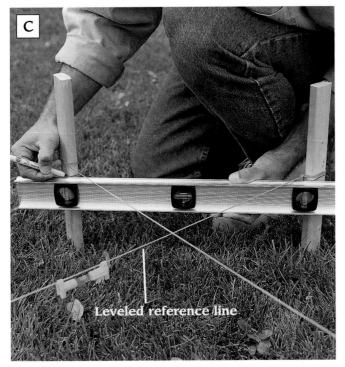

FIGURE C: Once one string line is exactly level, use it as a reference for leveling the rest of the strings, A carpenter's level can be used to transfer the height of the reference string line to adjacent string lines.

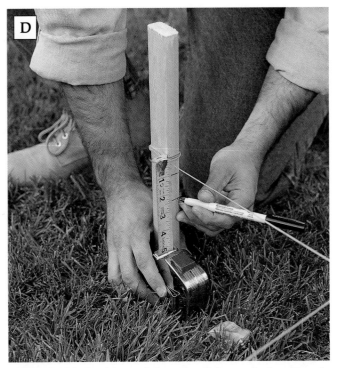

FIGURE D: Calculate how much the patio will drop on the low side and mark this distance below the level line marks on the low-side stakes. NOTE: Here we moved the string up and out of the way of the level reference line to make marking easier.

6 If the patio includes curved areas or rounded corners, lay out the curve with a garden hose, providing an 8-in. margin outside the actual curved edge of the patio **(See FIGURE F)**. On bare ground, mark the location with spray paint or pieces of paper with nails stuck through them. If your patio will replace a section of lawn, use the hose as a guide and remove the grass with a sod kicker.

Preparing the base

7 Starting at one corner, excavate the entire site to a depth that will accommodate at least 4 in. of subbase material, 1 in. of sand and the thickness of the pavers (for example, if the pavers are 2½ in. thick, you'd excavate to a depth of 7½ in. below the finished patio surface). Use a spade to dig the sides of the excavation as straight as possible, following your excavation marks. Check excavation depth around the perimeter by measuring down from the strings with a tape measure or a story pole **(See FIGURE G)**. Then remove the soil within the patio area with a shovel. Be sure the entire excavation area follows the drainage slope of the strings. *TIP: On larger patios, tie intermediate strings across the project site to provide more depth reference lines in the middle of the excavation.*

8 After excavating the site, use a long, straight 2 × 4 to check for low and high spots **(See FIGURE H)**. Fill any low spots with compactible gravel subbase and tamp firmly with a hand tamper.

FIGURE E: Remove sod within the patio area plus 6 to 8 in. beyond the layout lines using a sod kicker. Roll several strips (green side in), and keep it moist and shaded for later use to patch in around the patio.

9 Spread an even layer of compactible gravel subbase into the project area. The depth of the subbase should be 4 in. plus ½ in. to allow for compaction. Compact the subbase material with a plate vibrator or hand tamper around the patio perimeter, then move in overlapping passes toward the center of the excavated area, overlapping each pass by 4 in. **(See FIGURE I).** After compacting, double-check the height of the subbase to the guide strings. The distance between the subbase and strings should be equal over the whole

FIGURE F: Use a garden hose to plot curved corners of the patio for excavation. The hose should lay 6 to 8 in. outside the actual curve to allow for excavation and patio edging.

FIGURE G: Use a scrap wood story pole as a depth reference as you excavate. The marks on the pole indicate the depth of the excavation below grade, plus the distance between ground level and the string lines.

FIGURE H: Check for high and low spots in the excavated area with a straight 2 × 4. Remove or fill areas as needed and tamp the ground firmly with a plate vibrator or hand tamper to create a solid base.

FIGURE I: Fill the excavation area with a 4½-in.-thick layer of compactible subbase and compact it with a plate vibrator or hand tamper.

excavation area and follow the drainage slope marked by the reference string lines.

10 Lay down strips of landscape fabric, overlapping each strip by 6 to 8 in. (See FIGURE J). The fabric will help control weed growth and separate the sand layer from the compactible gravel subbase. Without it, the sand would eventually settle into the subbase material and cause the pavers to sink.

11 Starting at the center of the patio, dry-lay a line of pavers in both directions to establish the actual size of the finished patio (See FIGURE K). Be sure to include border pavers. Leave the two lines of pavers in place to serve as reference guides for installing the edging.

12 Using your layout lines as guides, install paver edging around the patio perimeter. When installed, the L-shaped edging is designed to hold the sand base and border pavers in place. Lay a level

FIGURE J: Roll out landscape fabric to cover the entire patio area. Overlap the fabric strips at least 6 to 8 in.

FIGURE K: Lay a line of pavers in each direction to establish the actual length and width of the patio. Make sure to include border pavers, if applicable, and allow for joints between each paver.

FIGURE L: Align the edging with the layout string lines using a carpenter's level. The vertical ledges of the paver edging should be flush with the outer edges of the pavers.

FIGURE M: Tack sections edging with 10-in. galvanized landscape spikes to establish curves in the patio layout. Once the curves are determined, space the spikes every 12 to 18 in. to lock the edging in place.

against the layout lines and adjust the edging until it is directly below the lines. Adjust the pavers until they butt up against the edging **(See FIGURE L).**

13 Install the edging by driving 10-in. galvanized landscape spikes through the predrilled holes in the edging. Place spikes 18 to 24 in. apart for straight sections, 12 to 18 in. apart for curved sections, or as specified by the manufacturer **(See FIGURES M and N).** Trim sections of the edging flange so that the edging fits around obstructions like steps **(See FIGURE O).**

14 After the edging is installed, remove the stakes and reference lines. Lay down 1-in-dia. pipes across the width of the patio, spacing them about 6 ft. apart, and lay a 1½-in.-dia. pipe across the center. Cover the patio area with a layer of sand **(See FIGURE P).** The pipes will serve as depth spacers for the sand base when it's leveled and smoothed. The wider center pipe will establish a gentle slope from the center of the patio to the sides (called crowning) so that water will not pool in the middle but shed to either side. Moisten the sand so it's wet but not soaked through.

FIGURE N: Anchor the straight sections of edging at each spike hole with 10-in. galvanized landscape spikes. Be careful that the edging doesn't shift out of alignment with the string layout lines.

FIGURE O: Trim the edging, if necessary, to fit around steps or other obstructions. Paver edging that you trim should be supported from behind to keep these border areas rigid.

FIGURE P: Lay spacer pipes across the patio area (widthwise) and cover the patio area with a layer of sand. Settle the sand by dampening it with water. The pipes serve as spacers to crown and even out the sand layer.

FIGURE Q: Screed the sand layer with a straight 2 × 4 using two pipes at a time as runners under the screed board. Then tamp the sand with a hand tamper to pack it firmly.

15 Set a straight 2 × 4 screed board across the sand that is long enough to rest on both the wider center spacer pipe and a narrower pipe. Shuffle it side to side along the two pipes in a sawing motion as you pull it toward you **(See FIGURE Q).** Continue screeding across sets of pipes, working from the center of the patio area outward until you've smoothed the whole patio. As you go, fill in any low spots and remove excess sand that builds up in front of the screed board.

Laying the pavers

16 Starting at one corner (nearest to the house or at the high end of the patio), lay the first border paver tight against the edging. Use a rubber mallet or hammer and short wood block to set the paver into the sand **(See FIGURE R).**

17 Lay a row of border pavers 2 to 3 ft. in each direction from the corner along the edging, and

FIGURE R: Set the first paver into one corner of the edging. Tap it lightly with a rubber mallet or a hammer and a block of wood to bed it into the sand base.

FIGURE S: Establish your paver pattern by laying a 2- to 3-ft. row of border pavers, then fill the border area in. Bed the pavers into the sand with a mallet and check the flatness of the paver surface with a level or straightedge.

fill in the space with field pavers following the paver pattern you choose **(See FIGURE S).** Tap the pavers in place, checking frequently with a level or straightedge to make sure all pavers are at the same height. As you encounter spacer pipes, remove them, filling in the grooves left behind with sand and lightly patting these areas smooth.

18 Continue laying the border and field pavers in 2- to 3-ft. sections diagonally across the patio area. As you work, measure from paver rows over to the edging to make sure the rows are lining up with one another. Compensate for inconsistencies by increasing or decreasing the joint width between pavers to bring a row back into alignment. When you get to the opposite end of the patio, adjust the edging, if needed, so it is snug against the pavers **(See FIGURE T).**

19 If your pattern requires you to cut only a few pavers, you can score and break them with a hand maul and brick set. If you have several dozen cuts to make or need to make angled cuts, rent a masonry saw (See *TIP,* above). These saws feature a water-cooled diamond-grit blade and a sliding carriage for moving the paver into the blade. Some models include a miter guide attached to the carriage that enables you to make angled cuts. Simply align the paver cutting line with the saw blade and slide the movable saw carriage forward, easing the paver slowly into the blade.

20 When your patio design includes a curve, lay full-size border pavers into the curve first, then fill in the field with full pavers as close to the border curve as possible **(See FIGURE U).** If you're

FIGURE T: Continue to add pavers until you reach the opposite end of the patio. If paver rows extend beyond the edging or come up short, shift the edging by removing and repositioning the stakes to avoid cutting border pavers.

FIGURE U: Lay the border pavers first in curved corners, then fill in the field area with full pavers as close to the curved border as possible. Field pavers that meet the border pavers at angles will have to be cut to fit.

FIGURE V: Mark full-size pavers that must be cut at angles by setting them over the empty spaces between border and field pavers and marking the angle. Allow for a ⅛-in. gap between border and cut pavers.

FIGURE W: Check the patio surface for flatness with a straight 2 × 4, and set high pavers deeper into the sand base with a mallet. In some cases, you'll need to remove low pavers, add sand and reset.

working into a tight radius, use half-pavers (cut across their width) for the border to minimize large, pie-shaped gaps that would result from laying full-sized pavers. Shortening the pavers tightens their fit into the radius.

21 Set full-size pavers over the empty spaces between field pavers and border pavers, and draw angled reference lines **(See FIGURE V).** Subtract

⅛ in. and make a second angled line inside the first to mark your cutting line. Cut or score and break the pavers along the inside line and fit them into place.

22 Once all the pavers are laid, check for high or low spots by laying the screed board across the paver surface in several directions and look for gaps. Use a rubber mallet or a hammer and wood block to adjust uneven pavers by setting higher pavers deeper

FIGURE X: Fill gaps between the pavers by covering the patio with a layer of sand and sweeping it back and forth into the joints. Use a plate vibrator to settle the entire patio into the sand base and pack the sand into the joints.

FIGURE Y: Sweep loose sand off the patio and settle the sand in the joints by misting with a garden hose.

into the sand **(See FIGURE W).** Remove any pavers in low spots, add more sand and reset them.

23 Spread an even ½-in. coat of dry sand over the entire paver surface. Sweep the sand thoroughly into the paver joints to fill them, adding more dry sand if necessary **(See FIGURE X).** Leave a ¼-in. layer of sand on top of the patio to act as a cushion for tamping the pavers with a plate vibrator. This will keep the vibrator from chipping the paver corners.

24 Tamp the pavers into the sand bed. Start around the outside perimeter and work toward the center. Make at least two passes to pack the sand firmly into the joints. If you notice joints settling, add more sand to refill them before making the next tamping pass. During this process, keep the tamper moving: if you stay in one place too long, you'll run the risk of creating uneven low spots by over-compacting the subbase.

25 Sweep up any loose sand, then mist the paver area, being careful not to dislodge sand from the joints **(See FIGURE Y).** Wait several days for the sand to settle and dry, then sweep in and wet additional sand to fill in any voids in the joints.

26 Fill in bare spots around the patio perimeter with topsoil, then cut strips of sod to cover the bare spots **(See FIGURE Z).** Press the sod firmly in place and soak it with water. Water the sod daily for two weeks so that it can establish new roots.

FIGURE Z: Fill excavated areas behind the patio edging with topsoil and patch it in with sod strips. Press the sod firmly into place and water it every day for several weeks until it takes root.

27 After the joints are fully packed with sand, the patio is ready for use. However, you may want to coat the paver surface with concrete sealer, using a roller or garden sprayer. The sealer not only provides some protection against water penetration and weed growth; it also enhances the color of the pavers and provides a barrier against stains and dirt. Check the sand joints seasonally and replenish them with sand. Reset low pavers as needed.

Before

Flagstone

Flagstone patios and walkways provide a durable if slightly rough walking surface, but lend themselves well to natural or informal garden settings. Because of their relatively large size and weight, flagstones usually don't require the extensive base preparation of an interlocking paver patio. In many cases, you can lay the stones directly on stable, well-tamped soil, although a 2 in. bed of screeded sand will make it easier to place and level stones of varying thickness. If the soil is very soft or unstable (subject to severe frost heave), lay down a 2 to 4 in. layer of compactible gravel subbase material, and compact it with a hand tamper or plate vibrator.

About flagstones

"Flagstone" is a general term referring to any sedimentary rock that cleaves naturally into stepping stone shapes. The name derives from the obvious resem-

Buying Flagstones

Rockeries and landscape suppliers generally sell flagstones by the ton (in pallet lots) for large projects, or by the pound for smaller ones. The stones in any given lot will vary in size, shape, and thickness, making estimating difficult. To determine the amount of stone needed to cover your walk or patio area, your best bet is to rely on the experience of the supplier.

Flagstones used for patios and walks range from 1 to 2 in. thick (as opposed to thinner "veneer" flagstones, which range from ¼ to ¾ in. thick—the latter should not be used for patios or walks). Generally, a ton of 1- to-2 in.-thick, medium-density stones will cover approximately 120 square feet.

After determining the square footage of your patio, order 10% extra to allow for cutting, fitting and breakage. While dealers usually won't let you pick through the pile to choose the exact stones you want, you can look for pallets that contain a good mixture of sizes and shapes to save time cutting and fitting. Also, a good percentage of the stones should have at least one reasonably straight side for use as perimeter stones on square or rectangular patios and straight walks.

As with other patio materials, have the stones delivered as close to the site as possible. Have a helper on hand to move and place the larger stones.

In formal landscapes, where a more symmetrical patio is desired, use "gauged" stones. These are natural stones split to roughly the same thickness, then cut into rectangular shapes in random widths and lengths. Gauged-stone patios are generally easier to fit together, with straight, wet-mortared joints of an even width (typically ½ to ¾ in. wide). Alternatively, you can lay these stones without mortar joints, using the same procedures as you would for installing the interlocking paver patio described on pages 22 to 29.

---

blance to flag shapes exhibited by flagstones. Limestone, slate and quartzite are some of the most common rock types in the flagstone category—specific types vary according to geographic region. To be useful for creating walkways and patios, flagstones should be at least 1 in. thick, but at least 1½ to 2 in. is preferable. Because flagstones are split and cleaved into usable and manageable sizes (rather than cut), their shapes are slightly irregular, which contributes to their natural quality. When purchased at a landscape stone supplier, natural stones like flagstone are considerably more expensive than cast pavers.

Laying out flagstone structures

Laying stones for a flagstone patio or walkway is somewhat like putting together a jigsaw puzzle. You'll want to lay the stones in an eye-pleasing pattern, while at the same time fitting them together to minimize the number of cut stones needed. Generally, the thickest stones are laid around the perimeter, serving as a border to help keep the thinner field stones in place. The largest stones are sometimes placed near the center of the patio. Strive for a pattern that includes a good mixture of large and small stones, placed in a random pattern, with staggered joints. For the most part, the larger

stones are laid and leveled first, then the smaller stones are fitted in between the larger ones. This allows you to limit any cutting to the smaller stones.

Installing flagstones

Before laying in the base materials, you can experiment with different patterns to make best use of the stones. Starting at one corner or side, test-fit various stones to find the best pattern without having to make too many cuts. You don't need to dry-lay the entire patio or walkway, but you should at least play around with the shapes enough to develop a feel for how they naturally fit together. If you do dry-lay the entire arrangement, either number the stones before moving them or keep the dry-lay intact, transplanting the stones one-at-a-time into the actual work site. Another option is simply to take a photograph of the dry-lay and use it as a reference for recreating the arrangement in the work site. Strive to keep the joints between the stones from ½ in. to not more than 1½ in. wide.

Even medium-sized flagstones can weigh 100 pounds or more, so make sure to get plenty of help handling them. Doing careful planning and base preparation will minimize the number of times you need to handle each stone.

Flagstone patios

Before laying in the base materials for your patio, experiment with different patterns to make best use of the stones. Mark any stones that will need to be cut. Draw a rough sketch of the layout to show where the stones will be placed. You might also find it helpful to number the stones with a pencil or piece of chalk to indicate their location, then cross-reference these to your sketch. Remove and stack them in small piles outside the patio area, near where they will be laid.

Excavate the project area

1 If you're building a square or rectangular patio, lay out the patio outline with stakes and leveled strings as described in the paver patio project on pages 22-29. Be sure to adjust the strings to provide the proper ⅛-in.-drop-per-ft. slope to facilitate water runoff from the patio surface, especially if the patio will adjoin a building. If you're laying a free-form design such as the one shown in this project, drive stakes every 3 to 4 ft. around the perimeter to indicate the border. Prepare the project area by removing all obstacles and sod, then excavate to a depth that will accommodate the thickest flagstones plus 4 in. of compactible gravel sub-base and 2 in. of sand **(See FIGURE A).** Run leveled strings across the excavation (from stake to stake) in several directions, and measure down from these to make sure the bottom of the excavation follows the intended slope of the finished patio. Then tamp it firmly with a hand tamper or plate vibrator.

Prepare the base

2 Install landscape edging around the patio border to contain the subbase, then pour and spread an even layer of compactible gravel subbase into the excavation (the back side of a garden rake works well for this). The depth of the material should be at least 4 in. plus ¼ to ½ in. to allow for compaction. Compact the material with a hand tamper, or for larger areas, a rented plate vibrator **(See FIGURE B).**

3 Lay down a layer of landscape fabric over the compacted base, overlapping the edges of the fabric at least 6 to 8 in. **(See FIGURE C).** Trim the edges to leave a 6-in. overlap beyond the patio borders.

4 Spread a 2- to 3-in.-thick bed of coarse, dry sand into the excavation area. Level and smooth the sand with a 2 × 4 screed board **(See FIGURE D).** Then

HOW TO INSTALL A FLAGSTONE PATIO

FIGURE A: Drive stakes to indicate the borders of the patio, then excavate deep enough for the subbase, sand and flagstones (around 8 in. for most projects).

Landscape edging

FIGURE B: Fill the project area with a 4½-in.-thick layer of compactible subbase. Tamp it with a hand tamper or plate vibrator.

compact the sand with a hand tamper or plate vibrator. *TIP: For a more stable base, you can mix Portland cement into the sand before screeding (use one 90 lb. sack of dry Portland cement mix per 100 sq. ft. of patio surface). After laying the sand, spread the dry cement mix evenly onto the sand and blend it in with a rake or hoe.*

Lay the stones

5 Starting at one high side of the patio, lay all of the border stones around the patio perimeter. Avoid kneeling on the screeded sand bed—if you must do so, cut a 4 × 4 piece of plywood and use it as a kneeling board to help distribute your weight evenly **(See FIGURE E).** Use the thickest stones for the border, setting them a bit deeper than the rest to offset the extra thickness. Thicker, heavier border stones will help anchor the center (field) stones in place. Twist the stones slightly to bed them into the sand. Check the border stones with a level and adjust as needed to ensure that the desired drainage slope is maintained.

6 After the border stones are in place, arrange the stones to fill in the field area **(See FIGURE F).** Maintain a good mixture of large and small stones across the entire patio to create an even, attractive pattern. Strive to keep the joint width between the stones about ½ in. to 1½ in. Bed the stones into the sand with a rubber mallet or a hammer and wood block.

7 No matter how carefully you arrange the stones, some stones will need to be cut to fill in odd spaces. To cut the stones, mark the cutting lines with a pencil on both sides. Score the cutting line ⅛ in. deep with a circular saw fitted with a carborundum or diamond masonry blade. (You can use a hammer and brick set instead to score the stones.) Then tap back and forth along the score line with your hammer and brick set until the stone fractures **(See FIGURE G).**

8 After laying all the stones, recheck the entire surface to make sure the stones are reasonably close to the same height. Use a long 2 × 4 with a level attached to check for overall level and slope. Let the

FIGURE C: Cover the subbase with landscape fabric, overlapping the edges 6 to 8 in. Extend the fabric up the sides of the excavated area.

FIGURE D: Spread a 2-in. layer of sand over the landscape fabric and screed the sand flat with a straight 2 × 4. Be sure the surface follows the drainage slope of the patio.

FIGURE E: Set the border flagstones into place and twist them slightly to bed them into the sand base. Where possible, use the largest, thickest stones for the border. If you must work within the patio field area, kneel on plywood to keep from disturbing the sand base.

FIGURE F: Once you've positioned pavers around the patio border, fill in the field area. Let your larger stones dictate the layout and set them into the patio field area first. Then fill in remaining areas with smaller stones. Keep the width of the joints between stones to 1½ in. or less.

stones settle for a few days and then recheck the patio area for level and slope. If one or more stones have sunk lower than the rest, remove these and add more sand beneath **(See FIGURE H).** Remove sand under stones that are higher than the rest. Bed the stones firmly into the sand by tapping them with a rubber mallet or hammer and wood block. Be patient and do your best work at this dry-fit stage—this step is critical to the appearance of the finished patio.

Fill the joints

9 Fill the joints with dry mortar mix. To make the mortar, mix one part Portland cement to six parts coarse sand in a wheelbarrow or five-gallon bucket. Wet the entire patio surface by misting it with a hose, then allow the surfaces of the stones to dry. Pour the

dry-mortar mixture evenly over the patio surface and sweep it into the joints with a push broom **(See FIGURE I).** Compact the mortar into the joints with a 4-ft. length of 1 × 4, or a strip of plywood. (It's a good idea to wear gloves when you handle the mortar mix.) Repeat the process until the dry mortar is well-packed and flush with the stone surfaces. *NOTE: In colder climates where the ground freezes seasonally, use sand instead of mortar mix to fill the joints. Sweep sand into the joints and tamp it firmly.*

10 Mist the patio surface **(See FIGURE J)**, being careful not to wash the mortar from the joints. When the patio surface has dried out and the mortar has partially set (about one hour), repeat the joint-filling process, if necessary to fill any low spots. After all joints are flush, allow the mortar to set for several hours, then use a coarse, water-soaked rag or burlap sack and stiff bristle brush to clean off any excess mortar from the stone surfaces. Cover the entire patio with 4- or 6-mil plastic sheeting and allow the mortar to cure for at least two days. Do not walk on the patio during this time. After the mortar is fully cured, you can remove any remaining mortar stains from the stones by scrubbing with a light solution of one part muriatic acid to nine parts water (wear safety glasses, heavy rubber gloves and long sleeves).

JOINT OPTION: Ground cover

For a more natural looking patio, you can fill joints between the flagstones with topsoil, then plant grass or a low ground cover in the soil. Popular low ground covers for this purpose include dichondra, Scotch or Irish moss, baby tears, and woolly thyme, to name a few. Check with local nurseries for options that will be suitable for your climate.

FIGURE G: To cut stones, score along your cutting lines with a mason's chisel and hammer or with a circular saw and masonry blade set to ⅛ in. Tap along the score line until the stone breaks.

FIGURE H: Backfill with sand beneath low pavers. You may also need to remove some sand behind pavers that are higher than others. The goal is to create a flat flagstone surface overall.

FIGURE I: Sweep a dry mortar mixture of one part cement to six parts sand into the patio joints. Compact the joints with pieces of scrap wood.

FIGURE J: Set the joints by misting them with water. Fill any joints that settle with more mortar mix before the joints cure.

Loose Fill

Loose fill is used mostly for walkways, but can make a very effective patio material in the proper setting as well. Smaller aggregates, like river rock or quartz, are common loose-fill materials that are quite durable. But mulch, bark and other organic matter may be used instead. Organic matter will decompose eventually and require replenishing, but it is easy to work with, inexpensive, and has a natural warmth that cannot be achieved with stone.

To keep the loose fill confined to the project area, you'll need to install edging around the border of the project. There are several edging options to choose from, including those shown in the TIP on the next page. But one of the beauties of working with loose-fill is that you can improvise by using your creativity to employ other materials for edging. Rubble stone from your yard, reclaimed bricks, chunks of logs, and pieces of salvaged fence material are just a few possibilities.

While ease of installation and natural beauty are two big advantages to creating loose fill walkways and patios, perhaps the greatest advantage is that they conform easily to curves, serpentine shapes, and other non-linear forms—with no time-consuming cutting of pavers or flagstones. And if you decide to alter the layout of your landscape, a loose-fill walkway or patio is easy to relocate.

LOOSE FILL OPTIONS

Loose fill for landscaping projects can be created from just about any natural material. Smaller aggregates, mulch and bark are the most common, however. Examples shown above are: (A) crushed limestone; (B) ⅜ to ¾ in. dia. river rock; (C) cypress mulch and; (D) cedar bark chips.

TOOLS FOR BUILDING A LOOSE-FILL WALKWAY

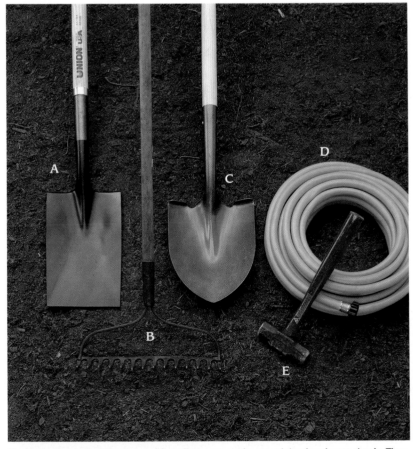

Tools needed to build a loose-fill walkway or patio are minimal and very simple. They include: (A) square-nose spade; (B) garden rake; (C) standard spade; (D) garden hose; and (E) hand maul for driving layout stakes.

Edging Options

Concrete pavers laid on their sides create stable edging that resists decay and adds a formal flavor to the pathway or patio, especially if there are other paver structures in the vicinity of the walkway or patio.

Landscape edging is the most common edging treatment for loose-fill walkways and patios. It is inexpensive and bends easily to follow curves. Avoid cheaper versions of this product that are flimsy and not designed to be staked in place.

Exterior lumber, such as cedar, redwood or pressure-treated pine makes excellent edging for straight borders.

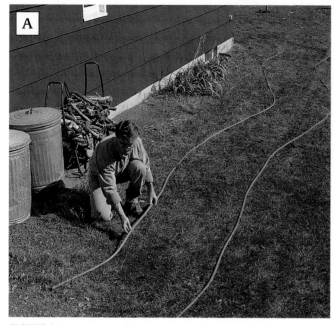

FIGURE A: Lay out curved walkways with lengths of garden hose or heavy rope. Keep the width of the walkway uniform, even around curves.

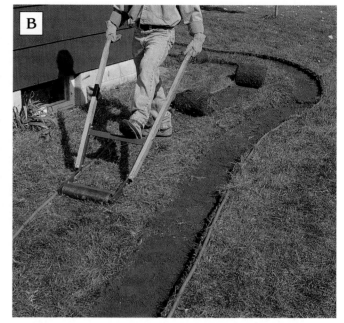

FIGURE B: Remove sod within the layout area using a rented sod kicker. Then excavate the walkway area to a depth of 3 to 4 in.

Loose-fill walkways

1 For straight walks, set up stakes and strings to outline the walkway area, as you would for a patio. For curved walks, lay out the area using a garden hose or rope **(See FIGURE A).** Be sure to include a margin on each side to allow for the width of the edging you'll install, if using heavier edging materials like pavers or pressure-treated wood.

2 If the walkway will cross a lawn, remove the sod with a sod cutter **(See FIGURE B).** On bare ground, remove all plantings and other obstacles within the walkway area (although you're better off designing the walkway to wind around them). Then, remove topsoil in the area to a depth of 3 to 4 in. below grade, and tamp the bottom of the excavation with a hand tamper or plate vibrator. If the soil is very loose or sandy, you may need to install a compactible gravel subbase, as you would for a paver patio.

3 Dig a shallow trench along the walkway edges for the edging material **(See FIGURE C).** The bottom of the edging should extend about 2 in. below the excavated area. The top of the edging should be about 1 in. above ground level to prevent soil from washing into the walkway, and ½ in. above the finished walk surface to contain the aggregates.

4 If you're using plastic edging, install it on both sides of the excavated walk area. Installation techniques will vary, depending on the brand of edging used. In this case, we drove galvanized stakes through a flange on the strip to secure the edging **(See FIGURE D)**.

5 As you lay successive plastic edging strips end to end, connect the ends according to the manufacturer's instructions. Here, the ends of the edging are coupled together with short sections of tubing **(See FIGURE E).**

6 Lay down a strip of landscape fabric to keep the loose fill from migrating into the soil beneath, and to prevent weed growth in the walkway area **(See FIGURE F).** Overlap the ends of the fabric 6 to 8 in. and drape it up over the sides of the excavated area. On tight curves, pleat the fabric neatly and secure it with 16d galvanized nails, poked through the material and into the ground.

7 Fill in the walkway area with 3 to 4 in. of loose aggregate material and rake it smooth **(See FIGURE G).** We used river rock for this project, but several aggregate options are widely available (See page 37). The finished walkway surface should be ½ to 1 in. below the edging.

8 Trim off excess landscape fabric or plastic sheeting with a pair of scissors or a utility knife **(See FIGURE H).** Replace the aggregate to hide any exposed fabric or plastic. Replenish the loose fill with fresh material as it settles or deteriorates.

FIGURE C: With a square-nose spade, dig shallow trenches along the edges of the walkway to provide for the edging you choose. Plan for the top of the edging to be 1 in. above the level of the surrounding ground.

FIGURE D: Install the edging. For this project, we used rolled plastic landscape edging that is held in place with galvanized stakes. Drive the stakes through the edging and into the ground.

FIGURE E: Lock lengths of plastic edging together with couplings provided by the manufacturer. This edging uses short sections of tubing.

FIGURE F: Cover the bottom of the excavation with a landscape fabric as a weed barrier material.

FIGURE G: Fill the walkway with 3 or 4 in. of loose aggregate material and smooth it with a rake. For heavier aggregates like rock, have the load dumped close to the worksite to make filling the walkway easier.

FIGURE H: Trim away excess landscape fabric or plastic sheeting and hide the edges with more aggregate.

Water gardens

Not too many years ago, the only way a homeowner could have a natural-looking garden pond was to pour a concrete shell to hold the water. Such ponds were—and still are—expensive and labor-intensive to build. And, if they're not installed correctly, with careful attention paid to climate and soil conditions, they'll soon develop cracks, causing leaks.

However, with the advent of flexible plastic and rubber pond liners, even large, elaborate ponds are well within the building capabilities of the home handyman. The liners are durable, cheaper than concrete, easy to install, and they enable you to create a pond of practically any size or shape. You can also use the liners to build natural-looking streams or waterfalls leading to the pond. Depending on the quality and thickness of the liner, a properly installed pond can last 30 years or more.

Preformed rigid plastic or fiberglass pond shells are another option for do-it-yourself water garden construction. They work especially well in soft, sandy or unstable soil, where any shifting, slippage, or erosion may deform the original shape of the hole beneath a flexible liner. However, sizes and shapes of preformed shells are limited. Also, unless carefully disguised with stone edgings and border plantings, the shells can have an artificial look, and may not be the best choice for a "natural-looking" pond. Conversely, those with geometric shapes and straight sides (squares, rectangles, circles, hexagons, etc.) better lend themselves to formal landscapes, where you might want to use bricks, patio tiles or pavers as edging materials.

Rigid shell liners, made from plastic or fiberglass, are usually buried below grade. But the shell above rests on the patio surface, where it is a real attention-getter.

All the bells and whistles of water garden design are displayed in this fanciful water garden project, including a multi-level waterfall, a charming footbridge, well-chosen water plants and decorative accessories, and even livestock (goldfish) inhabiting the main pond area.

In more formal settings, symmetrical shapes convey a sense of order, as shown by this flexible-liner pond. Rigid shell liners can be used for the same effect.

Integrating your pond with its surroundings is key to a successful water garden project, as shown by this pond that's recessed into a tiled patio.

This flexible-liner pond with waterfall relies on irregular coping stones and an abundance of water plants to achieve an easygoing, natural look.

Water Gardens   41

Flexible liner ponds

Installing flexible plastic or rubber pond liners is a quick and easy way to create a water garden. You simply outline the pond shape, dig the hole, install underlayment or a puncture-protection layer, lay in the liner to conform to the hole shape, fill the pond with water, then place stones (called *coping stones*) around the edges of the overhanging liner to make a border. Once you have all the materials on hand, you can easily build a modest garden pond in a single weekend. After the pond is installed, you can add a recirculating pump and filter to keep the water clear and healthy to support water plants and even livestock. You can give your pond a real custom flavor by adding a waterfall or a fountain.

Choosing a Liner

You have two basic choices in flexible pond liners: *PVC* plastic and *EPDM* (ethylene propylene diene monomer) or butyl rubber. Both types are designed to

flex and stretch to conform to the pond shape, and are resistant to ultraviolet (UV) radiation and nontoxic to fish and water plants.

Rubber liners outlast plastic ones (especially in cold climates where alternate freezing and thawing will eventually make plastic liners brittle), but are costlier. Both types come in different grades, depending on the thickness and material composition. PVC liners come in 20-mil and 32-mil thicknesses. Relatively new on the market are "enhanced" PVC liners (called *PVCE* in catalogs) that have better resistance to tears, punctures and UV radiation than conventional liners of the same thickness. Both the price and manufacturer's warranty are a good indication of the liner life. The same holds true for rubber liners, which come in 30- to 45-mil thicknesses. Premium rubber liners come with a bonded geotextile backing material to better resist tears and punctures. These are easier to install and come with a lifetime warranty. You can also buy the backing material separately to use as an underlayment beneath conventional plastic and rubber liners.

Sizing the Liner

You can buy flexible pond liners in a variety of stock sizes, as well as by the running foot in various widths. Whether you go with a stock size liner, or buy the material by running foot, estimate the amount you need as follows:

Step 1: After selecting the site (choose a site that's away from leaf-dropping trees and shrubs, and gets at least a half-day of full sunshine), clear the area of plantings and other obstructions, then outline the pond shape with a garden hose or heavy rope. For square or rectangular ponds, set up strings and batter boards, as you would to outline a deck or patio. These measurements represent the water surface of the pond only, not taking into account the width of any coping stones or materials.

Step 2: Measure the maximum length and width of the pond, then calculate the smallest rectangle that will enclose the overall length and width. Then determine the maximum depth of the pond (18 to 24 in. is optimum for raising fish and most aquatic plants).

Step 3: To calculate the required liner size, double the maximum depth, then add this figure to the width and length of the pond. Next, add the average width of the coping stones (typically 12 in.) and double this figure. *Example:* The pond fits inside a 6 × 8 ft. rectangle and is 24 in. deep in the center. The minimum liner width would be: 6 ft. (pond width) + 4 ft.(twice pond depth) + 2 ft. (twice the width of the coping stones) for a total width of 12 ft. The minimum liner length would be 8 ft. + 4 ft. + 2 ft. for a total of 14 ft. For this pond, you would need a liner approximately 12 × 14 ft. If your pond will include a waterfall, the pond liner should be large enough to extend up over the waterfall lip and partially into the first catch basin behind it. Order extra material to line the falls or the stream.

IMPORTANT NOTICE: **Because ponds and pools are drowning hazards, many municipalities require that any yard containing a permanent water feature be completely fenced in. Check with your local building inspector before starting your water garden project.**

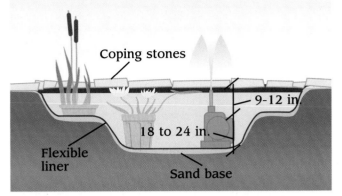

CROSS-SECTION OF A FLEXIBLE LINER POND

Coping stones

9-12 in.

18 to 24 in.

Flexible liner

Sand base

Flexible liner ponds in the 3 × 5 ft. to 4 × 6 ft. range should be 18 to 24 in. deep in the center to support water plants and livestock. A shallow shelf around the edge supports border plants, like cattails.

Installing a preformed shell liner

Installing a shell liner **(See Photo, page 41, top right)** is similar to installing a flexible liner in many ways. The soil should be free of stones, projecting roots and other sharp objects. Also, the excavation must be firmly tamped to prevent possible erosion from ground water that may create voids under the shell. If you're dealing with extremely loose or crumbly soil, or soils subject to frost heave or erosion from ground water, excavate the hole a bit larger to provide a firm, 4-in.-thick base of smooth pea gravel, topped by 2 to 3 in. of coarse sand, tamping firmly with a hand tamper.

To lay out the excavation area for a shell, place it on the ground, right-side up, then use a rope or garden hose and a plumb bob to transfer the outline of the pond shape to the ground beneath. Mark the outline with small stakes. Excavate the hole to conform to the shape of the pond shell, allowing an additional 2 to 3 in. around the sides and in the bottom for backfilling. Remove any stones, roots, or other sharp objects. Backfill the bottom of the hole, and other horizontal surfaces (such as ledges for plant shelves) with 2 to 3 in. of damp sand. Level the hole bottom. Test-fit the shell by setting it in into the hole. The shell rim should be about 1 in. above ground. Check the top of the shell for level with a 2 × 4 and carpenter's level. If necessary, lift out the shell and add or remove sand.

After you've leveled the shell, start filling the shell with water. As the water level rises, backfill around the shell with damp sand. Keep the sand even with the water level as it rises. After the pond is filled with water and the backfilling is complete, place coping stones or other coping materials around the pond perimeter to conceal the pond rim.

Installing a flexible liner pond

Test your soil before installing a flexible liner—if it's very sandy or silty, it may not be stable enough to support the liner. Either add a layer of compactible gravel, or choose a hard shell liner instead (See page 43).

Prepare the project area

1 Lay out your pond shape using an extension cord, garden hose or rope **(See FIGURE A)**. Remove sod within the layout lines and approximately 12 to 20 in. beyond them with a square-nosed spade. For large ponds (in excess of 50 sq. ft.), you may want to rent a sod kicker to make the job go more quickly. Level the area around the pond layout lines by removing or adding more dirt, and reestablish the layout lines as needed. *NOTE: When you design the shape of your pond, avoid sharp angles or too much symmetry in your layout. The more irregular and gentle the shape, the more natural the pond will look.*

2 Excavate within the layout lines to a depth of at least 9 in., sloping the sides of the hole about 20° from the edges of the excavation in toward the bottom. Check the hole depth by setting a carpenter's level on top of a long, straight 2 × 4. Lay the board across the excavation area in several directions, and measure down from the board to the bottom of the hole with a tape measure **(See FIGURE B)**.

3 Lay out a deeper center area of the pond around the bottom of the excavation area, as you did in *Step 1*. The borders should be 9 to 12 in. in from the walls of the hole. Dig out this center area to 20 to 26 in. deep, measuring down from ground level. Slope the walls 20° in toward the bottom of the excavation **(See FIGURE C)**. The resulting pond excavation should be a tiered hole with a 9 to 12-in.-wide upper "shelf" for aquatic plants.

4 Remove any sharp stones or protruding roots in the sides and bottom of the excavation area to minimize the risk of puncturing the liner. Smooth the cleared area outside the pond's perimeter and add or remove soil as needed to bring it to level. Check for level with a level and straight 2 × 4 **(See FIGURE D)**.

5 Spread a ½- to 1-in. layer of sand around the bottom of the excavation and on the plant shelf. The sand layer serves as a protective cushion under the pond liner **(See FIGURE E)**. Dampen the sand and tamp lightly with a hand tamper. Pack damp sand into voids left by any rocks or debris you removed from the pond walls.

HOW TO INSTALL A FLEXIBLE LINER POND

FIGURE A: Lay out the pond shape with a length of extension cord, garden hose or rope. Keep the shape somewhat asymmetric with gently rounding curves.

FIGURE B: Check the depth of the initial excavation area with a carpenter's level and a straight length of 2 × 4. Measure the depth at multiple points along the board and across several directions.

FIGURE C: Dig a smaller, 20 to 26-in.-deep section of the pond in the center of the first excavation area, leaving a 9 to 12 in.-wide plant shelf around the inside perimeter of the hole.

FIGURE D: Level off an area for coping stones around the edges of the pond excavation by adding or removing soil.

FIGURE E: Spread a layer of sand around the bottom of the hole and along the plant shelf. Dampen it and tamp lightly.

FIGURE F: Drape the pond liner over the pond excavation and press it into place so it conforms to the shape of the hole. Bricks or stones around the perimeter will help hold the liner in place.

FIGURE G: Fill the bottom of the excavation area with a 2-in. layer of clean pea gravel and smooth it with a rake or shovel. The gravel lends a natural look to the pond bottom and anchors potted aquatic plants.

FIGURE H: Fill the pond with water. Reposition the brick or stone liner hold-downs to allow the liner to shift and settle into its final shape.

FIGURE I: Trim extra liner away, allowing for a 9-in. overhang all around the pond rim.

Installing the flexible liner

6 Unfold the pond liner and place it in a sunny location for 15 to 20 minutes to warm it, which will help flatten it and make it more flexible. Drape the liner over the hole, overlapping it evenly on all sides of the

excavation area. Press the liner down so it roughly conforms to the shape of the hole and lays flat in the bottom—don't worry about wrinkles at this point; these will be smoothed out when you fill the pond with water. Crease the liner neatly around the perimeter of the hole and weight down the liner edges temporarily with smooth bricks or stones, spaced 1 ft. apart to hold the liner in place **(See FIGURE F).**

7 Spread a 2-in. layer of clean pea gravel over the deeper center excavation area and smooth it with a shovel **(See FIGURE G).** The gravel will give the pond bottom a more natural appearance and help hold potted aquatic plants in place.

8 Fill the pond with water, and readjust the bricks or stones that are holding the liner in place as the pond fills and the liner settles into shape **(See FIGURE H).** Do not kneel or stand on the liner. To determine the volume of your pond before you fill it, see *TIP,* left. As the pond fills, smooth the liner to remove smaller wrinkles. Fold or pleat large wrinkles to make them less obvious. Fill the pond to within 2 in. of ground level, then remove the brick or stone weights. Let the liner settle for a day.

9 Trim the excess lining around the pond perimeter, leaving a 9-to 12-in. overhang **(See FIGURE I).** The overhang forms a watertight edge around the pond and will be concealed by the coping stone border.

Estimating pond volume

There are several good reasons for knowing your pond's water volume. First, it will help you choose the correct size pump and filter if you plan to add one. Second, this information will help you determine dosages of various pond treatments, like algaecides and aquatic plant fertilizers, should the need arise.

Shortly before you're ready to fill up the pond for the first time, turn on the garden hose and record how long it takes to fill a 5-gallon bucket. Adjust the flow rate so the bucket fills up within an amount of time easily divisible into one minute (for example, 120 seconds). Then determine the flow rate: (5 gallons at 120 seconds divided by 2 equals 2.5 gallons per minute). Without changing the flow rate, place the hose in the pond and keep track of how long it takes to fill it up (say 45 minutes). Then multiply the gallons per minute by the number of minutes (2.5 gallons per minute times 45 minutes equals 112.5 total gallons).

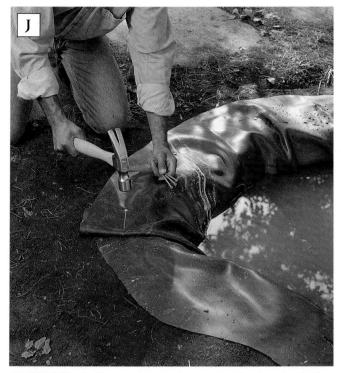

FIGURE J: Pin the liner overhang to the ground with 4-in. galvanized nails, spaced 12 to 18 in. apart.

FIGURE K: Dry-lay large, wide coping stones around the rim of the pond and fill in behind them with smaller stones. Overhang the front edges of the stones nearest the rim by 2 in.

10 Secure the liner overhang by driving 4-in. galvanized nails through it and into the ground about 3 to 4 in. in from the liner edge, spaced 12 to 18 in. apart **(See FIGURE J).** The nails will help hold the liner in place while you position the coping stones.

Lay the coping stone border

11 Dry-lay the coping stones around the pond perimeter so they overhang the pond by approximately 2 in. **(See FIGURE K).** For pointers on buying coping stones, see *TIP,* page 48. Try different coping stone arrangements until you find one that pleases you. For best drainage, identify the direction you want to direct water runoff and set the stone that's nearest that spot slightly lower than the rest of the coping stones. Use large, wide stones closest to the pond rim for stability, and fit smaller stones in between and behind the larger stones. Try to keep joint widths between stones to 2 in. or less. *NOTE: If you use flagstones, as we do for this project pond, it's relatively easy to cut them, should you need to. See page 33 for more information on cutting flagstones.*

12 While you can lay relatively large, flat stones directly over the liner without further anchoring, it's usually better to mortar the stones in place to keep them from slipping into the pond. Mix two parts sand to one part dry mortar in a wheelbarrow, using a shovel or hoe **(See FIGURE L).** *NOTE: Wear protective gloves when working with mortar.* Mist the mixture

FIGURE L: Prepare a mortar mix of two parts sand to one part dry mortar and mist with water. The mix should be just wet enough throughout to stick together and hold its shape. Lay a thick bed of the mortar mix around the perimeter of the pond to seat the coping stones. Try to keep the mortar at least 2 to 3 in. away from the edge of the pond.

FIGURE M: Spread a 2-in.-thick bed of mortar around the rim of the pond and set the coping stones into place. Pack mortar into the joints between stones.

TIP: Choosing coping stones

While you can use almost any type of rocks for coping stones, those with relatively smooth, flat surfaces and uniform thickness are the easiest to lay. Avoid stones with sharp edges that could puncture the liner. If you use field stones, make sure they have at least one relatively flat side, which should be placed flat-face down on the liner.

If you choose flagstone (as shown in this project), select stones that are at least 1 in. thick and at least 10 in. wide so they are able to overhang the pond edges by a few inches and hide the liner—without falling into the water. Consider building up several layers of flagstones, stacking them on top of one another and staggering the joints. Step each layer back slightly to help hold the stones in place.

FIGURE N: Smooth and brush away excess mortar from the joints with a damp paint brush. Work carefully to keep mortar from falling into the pond.

with water and mix it thoroughly—the mortar mix proportions are correct when you can form it into a ball in your palm and it retains the shape.

13 Spread a 2-in.-thick bed of mortar over the pond liner to within 2 in. of the pond rim. Set the coping stones into the mortar bed, twisting them slightly to seat them in the mortar **(See FIGURE M).** If you are using large, flat stones, such as flagstones, angle them back from the pond rim to direct water runoff away from the pond. Pack the joints between the stones full with mortar, and extend the joints to within 2 in. of the pond rim.

14 Smooth the mortar joints and sweep away excess mortar with a paint brush dampened with water **(See FIGURE N).** Allow the mortar to fully cure (about 5 to 7 days in dry weather). Scrub the stones and mortar edging with distilled white vinegar to neutralize the lime in the mortar. Rinse the stones with clean water and a sponge.

Filters, Fountains & Falls

In their most basic forms, small garden ponds can look quite plain—little more than a glorified mud puddle. It's adding your own unique details, like water plants, fountains and even waterfalls, that transform a basic pond into a unique landscape element.

Filtration systems. Most small garden ponds don't absolutely need a pump/filtration system once a biological balance has been achieved. But, if you want reasonably clear water for viewing fish and other aquatic life, it's a good idea to install one. A correctly sized pump and filter will also enable the pond to support a larger population of fish; for certain types, such as koi, filtration is essential.

Filters fall into two basic types: *mechanical* and *biological*. Both types clarify water by trapping particulate matter, such as floating algae, fish wastes and leftover fish food, dirt and organic matter, which cause cloudy water. Biological filters, and some mechanical ones, will also remove ammonia and other toxic chemicals.

Most homeowners with small backyard ponds (1,000 gallons or less) opt to install an in-pond mechanical filter with a matching pump. These employ a replaceable corrugated polyester cartridge (similar to those used in automobile oil filters) or a foam filter wrap. Other in-pond units combine the pump and filter in a single unit, and have replaceable filter pads. These filters are sized by maximum gallon capacity of the pond (for ponds up to 600 gallons, for example). Mechanical filters require frequent cleaning (every few days during the summer months), and high flow rates (larger pumps) to operate efficiently.

Water fountains are basically vertical attachments to recirculating pumps. Choose one with a spray pattern and water volume that's in proportion to your pond.

FILTERS & PUMPS

Submersible pumps are available in a wide range of sizes and with varying abilities to recirculate water for waterfalls and fountains. Some are sold with attachments for fountains. Read the package labeling carefully, and see the TIP on page 46 to determine which size pump your pond requires. The machine above is an external, biological filtration pump.

Waterfalls. Many garden ponds benefit by the addition of a waterfall. You can either buy a preformed watercourse, made of the same materials as preformed ponds, or use a flexible liner. Designs are as unique as the ponds into which they fall, and are largely a matter of personal taste. However, here are a few pointers to keep in mind:

• The most natural-looking waterfalls and streams consist of a series of two or more small catch basins or level areas connected by short cascades. For streams, a 1 to 2 in. drop per 10 feet is all that's required to make the water run downhill. This approach assures that some water will remain in the stream bed or catch basins when the pump is turned off.

• Use large, flat, overhanging rocks for the lip of the falls; this enables the water to fall directly into the pond with minimal water loss. A hollow area behind the falls amplifies the sound of splashing water as it falls into the pond.

• Placing small rocks and gravel in the streambed provides a more natural watercourse, and also helps protect the liner from the damaging effects of sunlight.

• As with ponds, the coping or edging stones along the bank can be mortared in place to prevent them from shifting and to help prevent leaks or runoff.

• If you're dealing with flat ground, use the soil excavated from the pond to build a mound or berm; use additional soil if necessary. Tamp the berm firmly to prevent erosion or slippage. On sloped sites, excavate flat steps or terraces for the pools or catch basins. Leave enough space to install coping stones. Dig the catch basins, leaving a 12-to 16-in. lip between them to form the connecting waterfalls. Install the liner over

Waterfalls help keep pond water healthy by creating aeration as the water flows and is reintroduced into the major pond basin. They're also beautiful and relaxing to watch and to listen to.

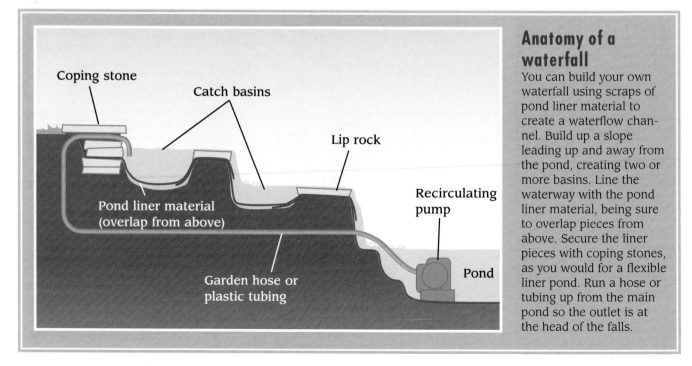

Coping stone

Catch basins

Lip rock

Pond liner material (overlap from above)

Recirculating pump

Pond

Garden hose or plastic tubing

Anatomy of a waterfall

You can build your own waterfall using scraps of pond liner material to create a waterflow channel. Build up a slope leading up and away from the pond, creating two or more basins. Line the waterway with the pond liner material, being sure to overlap pieces from above. Secure the liner pieces with coping stones, as you would for a flexible liner pond. Run a hose or tubing up from the main pond so the outlet is at the head of the falls.

the catch basins, following the same procedures as for a flexible liner pond. To finish the falls, install the pump and run the outlet tubing up alongside the falls to the top catch basin. Turn on the pump and make any final adjustments to the stones at the waterfall lip. If desired, you can bury the outlet tubing under a few inches of soil to help conceal it.

For a waterfall, you can buy a pump only, or a pump and filter. In all cases, you'll need to choose a pump that puts out enough water at the top of the falls to provide a pleasing cascade. Generally, if you've designed the falls to be in proportion to the pond, a pump that recirculates ½ to ⅔ of the pond's total water volume per hour should be sufficient to operate the falls. For larger cascades, choose a pump that can recirculate the entire gallonage of the pond in 1 hour.

A few words on electrical requirements: Make sure the pump you buy is designed for use in ponds. Submersible pumps should have waterproof cords; all pumps used outdoors or near water must be connected to a weatherproof GFCI outlet or have a GFCI breaker wired into the circuit. Electrical outlets for plug-in-pumps must be placed at least 6 ft. away from the water. Pump manufacturers usually offer cords of several different lengths to fit various situations. Check local electrical codes for additional requirements.

The waterfall above was created by piling rocks at one edge of this flexible liner pond, then running plastic tubing up from a recirculating pump submerged in the pond.

Fountains. Fountains fall into two basic categories—sprays and statuary. *Spray fountains* consist of a jet nozzle or ring (similar to garden sprinkler heads) attached to the outlet pipe of a submerged pump placed in the pond. You can choose from a variety of ornamental spray patterns. When added to the pond, sprays aerate the water, providing oxygen for fish and other pond life. When choosing a spray, make sure it is in proportion to the size of the pond. If the spray is too large, gusts of wind can blow water outside the perimeter of the pond; also the falling water will disrupt a large portion of the water surface, making it hard to grow water plants or view aquatic life beneath the water. Likewise, fountains with delicate or bell-shaped spray patterns must be placed in wind-free locations to avoid disrupting the pattern.

Spray fountains are relatively simple to install; for most backyard garden ponds, you'd buy the fountain head or nozzle, all the required fittings, and a matched submersible pump as a complete system. Some units can be fitted with a diverter valve to operate a second water feature, such as a waterfall or another fountain. If you're installing a custom fountain, seek advice from a knowledgeable pond dealer or installer in choosing components. In all cases, the submersible pump you choose should either have a top-mounted outlet or discharge, or include an elbow fitting that enables you to attach a vertical extension pipe and fittings for the spray head. The pump should also include a filter

screen or prefilter attached to the inlet to prevent the jet nozzles from clogging.

Statuary fountains are often sold as completely self-contained units that include the statue (also called the *ornament*), an integral pedestal and water reservoir, and in some cases, a base, or riser, beneath the reservoir bowl. Typically, a small submersible pump is housed inside the hollow pedestal below the water level of the reservoir and connects to the statue via a short length of flexible plastic tubing. The pump cord runs through the hollow statue base, hidden from view. Actual installation procedures will vary slightly, depending on the fountain style: To install, follow the directions that come with the unit. As with other water features that require pumps, the pump cord must be connected to a GFCI outlet or circuit.

Heavier statues (over 75 pounds, or so) will require a concrete footing installed beneath the pond liner or shell to support the weight of the statue—if the statue isn't supported by a firm footing, its weight may puncture or tear the flexible liner or eventually crack the rigid shell. Before installing the liner or shell, lay down a poured concrete footing in the statue location, about 4 to 6 in. thick, extending 3 to 4 in. beyond the statue base on all sides. For lighter statuary, firmly tamp the ground beneath the liner. In all cases, add an underlayment material both beneath and on top of the liner or shell to cushion the statue base and help prevent punctures of the pond liner.

A mixture of lillies, bog plants, floating plants and submerged plants keep the aquatic environment in balance in this pond.

Feature plants add color and a tropical flavor to any water garden.

Water lillies are the staples of aquatic plants. They're available in hundreds of varieties with flowers in dozens of rich colors.

Stocking Your Water Garden

While some people prefer a clear water pond without fish or aquatic plants, most pond builders opt to include one or both to add beauty and interest to the waterscape. While it's possible to have a pond with plants only, or one with fish only, it's usually best to have a good combination of both, along with scavengers such as snails, tadpoles, or freshwater clams or mussels. Ponds that include a diversity of aquatic life in correct proportions will achieve a natural biological balance, which will reduce the need for chemicals to control algae and the larvae of various insects, such as mosquitoes. Fish and plants also rely on each other to provide nutrients and oxygen necessary for their mutual survival.

Aquatic plants fall into four general categories: *Water lilies* come in hundreds of different varieties, but are generally subdivided into two main groups: *tropical* (for warm climates) and *hardy* (for moderate to cold climates). Lilies are typically planted in pots in the deep areas of the pond. In addition to having beautiful, showy flowers, their broad, floating leaves provide shade to help control water temperature for fish and cut down on algae growth during the hot summer months.

Bog plants include water iris, cattails, pickerel rush, and lotus, to name a few. These are also called *marginal plants* because they're grown in shallower water, on marginal plant shelves around the pond perimeter, or in bog gardens adjacent to the pond. Some bog plants have showy flowers, while others are grown for their interesting foliage. Bog plants help hide the liner around the pond margin, for a more natural appearance.

Floating plants, as the name implies, require no soil to grow. Their buoyant leaves keep them afloat as their dangling roots draw nutrients directly from the pond water. Popular species include water fern, water hyacinth, water lettuce, and duckweed. These plants, too, provide shade for fish and reduce algae growth, but must be selected carefully and thinned out periodically, as some types can completely cover the entire water surface in short order during their growing season.

Submerged plants, also called *oxygenating grasses,* grow completely underwater. Popular species include cabomba, anachris, ceratophyllum and vallisneria—the same types used in indoor aquariums. While they may not even be visible in the pond, submerged plants play a significant utilitarian role by providing oxygen for fish, and consuming nutrients (fish waste) that would otherwise promote algae growth. In larger ponds, submerged plants also provide a food source and spawning area for fish. Plant oxygenating grasses in pots to keep them anchored on the pond bottom; plastic bird netting secured over the leaves will prevent overgrazing by fish.

The most popular fish for ponds include goldfish, koi, and mosquito fish (the latter are small guppy-like fish, so named for their voracious appetite for mosquito larvae). All are cold-water fish (as opposed to tropical fish) because they adapt well to a wide variety of water temperatures. Tropical fish (such as those sold at pet stores) and game fish (trout, bass, catfish, bluegill, etc.) are generally not recommended for backyard ponds.

In addition to fish, you may want to add a few scavengers to the pond—water snails, tadpoles or pollywogs, and perhaps a few freshwater clams or mussels. Scavengers serve as the pond's "vacuum cleaner system," consuming fish waste, algae, and decaying plant matter, transforming these materials into nutrients for plants, and helping clarify the water. Pollywogs and tadpoles also hold a special fascination for children, as they eventually grow legs and turn into frogs.

The size and number of fish, plants, and other aquatic life you can grow in a pond depends on a variety of factors—available oxygen, sunlight and nutrients,

Planting aquatic plants

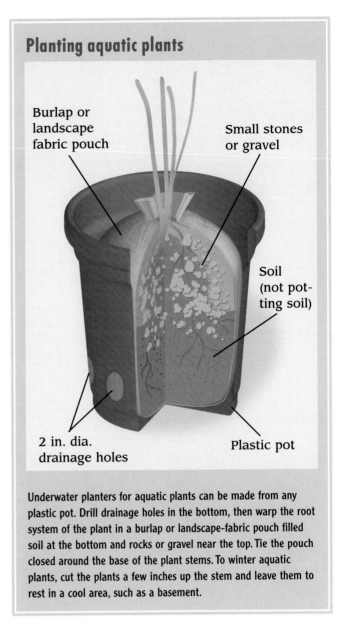

Burlap or landscape fabric pouch

Small stones or gravel

Soil (not potting soil)

2 in. dia. drainage holes

Plastic pot

Underwater planters for aquatic plants can be made from any plastic pot. Drill drainage holes in the bottom, then warp the root system of the plant in a burlap or landscape-fabric pouch filled soil at the bottom and rocks or gravel near the top. Tie the pouch closed around the base of the plant stems. To winter aquatic plants, cut the plants a few inches up the stem and leave them to rest in a cool area, such as a basement.

and the amount of water circulation and filtration provided by the pump and filter, if any. (The use of pumps and filters not only helps clarify the water, but enables you to support a larger population of fish and plants). In all cases, no two ponds are exactly alike, so the process of establishing a good ecological balance will be a matter of trial and error.

Before stocking the pond, wait several days for the "free chlorine" in the tap water to dissipate. Then, test the water with a test kit, available from water garden catalogs, pond and swimming pool dealers and pet shops. Simple kits test for pH (acidity or alkalinity) and levels of chlorine; others may include tests for ammonia, chloramines, nitrates, and water hardness. Or, you can take a sample of the water to a local pool dealer. After the water is balanced, add the plants, then wait a week or two for them to get established and oxygenate the water before stocking the pond with livestock.

Wall Structures

Walls serve a multitude of purposes in landscape construction, including retaining walls that prevent erosion and level off slopes, short walls built in a frame configuration to create raised planting beds, freestanding garden walls that divide a yard and border walls that define the boundaries of your property. From a visual standpoint, walls are key elements to a landscape design. They introduce new textures, define space and create vertical lines for visual interest.

Most walls are built using natural stone or concrete-based products, but you can also use landscape timbers for ease of workability and a softer appearance. Interlocking concrete blocks have become a very popular building material for walls, especially retaining walls and planting beds that contain earth. These artificial products are now available in a range of sizes, shapes and colors to give you plenty of design options. Hollow-core concrete construction blocks can also be used for building landscape walls, but they lack the texture and ease of installation of interlocking blocks designed specifically for outdoor and garden building purposes. Natural stone, such as rubble stone or fieldstone, is used to build all types of landscape walls, both dry-laid and mortared.

Wall structures 3 ft. in height or shorter pose no particular building problems for the do-it-yourselfer. Taller walls, however, usually need to be designed by a qualified professional, such as a landscape architect or soils engineer. Regardless of whether they're used as retaining walls, walls over 3 ft. high generally require building permits and fully-developed structural drawings.

Many wall building projects will require excavation and grading of the building area. Especially if you're building a large retaining wall into a steep slope, look into hiring a contractor to perform the earth moving chores (or, if you're at all experienced with earth moving equipment you can rent a small front end loader or skid—but be sure to contact your local public utilities first to have them check for any buried cables or pipes in the work area).

Interlocking concrete blocks are a very do-it-yourselfer friendly building material. They're generally cast with a flange on the lower back edge that slips behind the block beneath it, holding the wall together and creating a slight backwards slope that is intended to help the wall withstand the force of the earth pressing against. The retaining walls shown to the right demonstrate one of the best features of interlocking concrete blocks: they can easily be stacked to follow curves.

Landscape timbers are made from pine that is pressure-treated with rot-resisting chemicals. The 5×6 in. timbers to the right are joined together with pieces of steel rebar to form a planting bed or a shorter retaining wall.

Rough-hewn timbers are used to build posts and heavy-duty stringers that create support for the split-log vertical members in this unique retaining wall project. The posts and stringers are joined with half-lap joints reinforced with galvanized landscape spikes driven toe-nail style through the posts and into the stringers.

Raised planting beds break up flat lawns and help focus attention on your favorite feature plants. Interlocking concrete blocks represent an easy and effective solution to building planting beds.

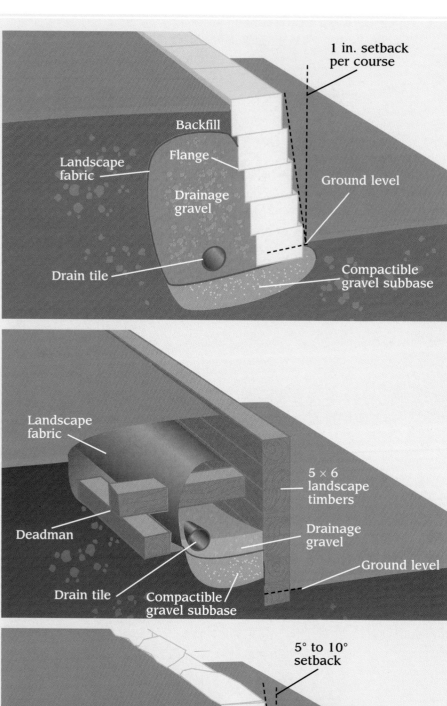

1 in. setback per course

Backfill

Landscape fabric

Flange

Drainage gravel

Ground level

Drain tile

Compactible gravel subbase

Interlocking block retaining walls

Interlocking concrete blocks are stacked in staggered courses, beginning with half of the first block below grade. Half-blocks are used at the ends of alternating courses. Blocks with flanges on the back lower edges are overlapped to tie the wall together. Some blocks are pinned together with nylon pins (called keys). Construction adhesive is applied between courses for extra holding power. A course of thin capstones can be installed at the top of the wall to conceal the gaps between interlocking blocks.

Landscape fabric

Deadman

Drain tile

Compactible gravel subbase

5 × 6 landscape timbers

Drainage gravel

Ground level

Timber retaining walls

Landscape timbers are stacked together, with the first timber course below grade. Subsequent courses are joined with landscape spikes or pieces of steel rebar. Weep holes for drainage are drilled in the lower courses, and sometimes created by leaving slight gaps at end joints between timbers. About ⅔ up the wall, a timber with an attached cross piece (called a deadman) is installed perpendicular to the wall every 4 to 6 ft. The deadmen anchor the wall to the hill. See Page 71.

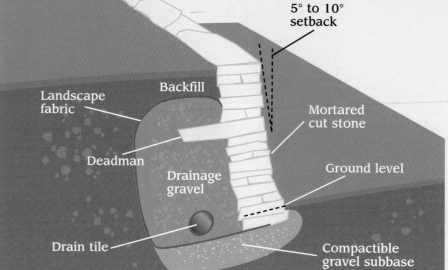

5° to 10° setback

Backfill

Landscape fabric

Deadman

Drainage gravel

Drain tile

Mortared cut stone

Ground level

Compactible gravel subbase

Cut stone (ashlar) retaining walls

Cut sedimentary stones (sometimes called ashlar stones) are mortared together in courses. The first course is set below grade, sloping slightly from front to back. This creates a cant in the wall, allowing it to utilize gravity to counteract the pressure of the earth behind it. Longer stones are inserted in the deadman position, as with timber retaining walls. On the second or third course above grade, sections of 1 to 2 in. pipe are inserted into the gaps between stones every 6 to 8 ft. for drainage.

Retaining Walls

From a functional standpoint, retaining walls serve to prevent soil erosion on hillsides and to create usable flat spaces on sloping lots. If you're faced with a steep slope, it's often easier and more attractive to install a series of low terraced walls, rather than one tall one. Terracing provides space for a series of raised planting beds or walkways (See Illustration, right).

A slope doesn't necessarily have to be steep to benefit from the addition of a retaining wall. For example, low walls can be built simply to prevent water runoff from a gently sloping lawn onto a sidewalk or driveway. Low retaining walls can also serve as decorative boundary markers to discourage people and animals from cutting across your lawn area.

The basic site preparation, excavation, and installation of base and backfill materials are essentially the same for all types of retaining walls—regardless of building material. The wall footing consists of a trench filled with tamped compactible gravel. The excavated space behind the wall is covered with landscape fabric, then filled with coarse gravel or river rock; a perforated drain pipe at the base of the wall further promotes drainage. In poorly draining soil, you may also want to dig a swale on the uphill side of the wall, about 2 ft. back from and parallel to the wall. A swale is a shallow trench about 2 ft. wide and 6 to 8 in. deep designed to slow the flow of rushing water runoff and help direct it away from the wall.

The way you treat the retaining wall ends should depend on the angle and direction of the slope, the desired drainage patterns, and surrounding features on your property. To prevent soil erosion at each end of the wall, you may need to turn the wall back into the hillside or slope. The sidewalls can meet the front wall at a sharp 90° angle, or they can be curved back gently, or tapered back at a shallow angle. To reduce the number of blocks needed for the sidewalls, dig a stepped trench between the front wall and the top of the slope. Extend the sidewalls as far back as necessary to contain the slope or create the desired amount of flat space above the retaining wall.

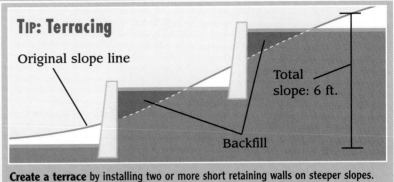

Tip: Terracing

Original slope line

Total slope: 6 ft.

Backfill

Create a terrace by installing two or more short retaining walls on steeper slopes. Terracing reduces the amount of dirt you'll need to move and backfill, and keeps wall heights to a manageable 3 ft. or less.

TOOLS & MATERIALS FOR BUILDING WALL STRUCTURES

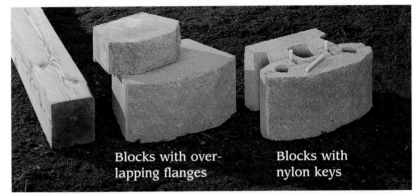

Blocks with overlapping flanges

Blocks with nylon keys

Landscape timbers and interlocking concrete blocks can be used to make landscape walls for just about any purpose. Timbers range in size from 4 × 4 to 8 × 8 (5 × 6 is shown above). Interlocking blocks, sold in a range of sizes, styles and colors, are connected either with overlapping flanges or with nylon keys.

Tools for building landscape walls include: (A) rubber mallet; (B) hand maul; (C) 4-ft. level; (D) circular saw with masonry-cutting blade; (E) combination blade for cutting wood; (F) hand tamper; (G) spade; (H) 50-ft. roll tape; (I) tape measure; (J) caulk gun; and construction adhesive; (K) corded drill with spade bits and bit extender; (L) brickset; (M) mason's line.

Interlocking block

Today, most residential and commercial wall structures are made of interlocking concrete blocks. Sometimes called gravity walls, these interlocking systems usually require no concrete footings, and can be built without mortar.

The blocks come in many different sizes, textures and colors. Correctly installed, interlocking block walls are exceptionally durable and maintenance free. The modular blocks require little skill to install. Some types are solid, with predrilled holes in which you install nylon or fiberglass connecting pins (keys) to lock the courses together; others have hollow cores and built-in flanges to hold them in place; the cores are filled with a backfill material (crushed rock or gravel) to stabilize the wall and promote drainage.

The blocks are designed with a built-in setback to better resist soil and water pressure behind the wall. Most types are also self-draining, so no weep holes are required. They accommodate themselves to straight or curved (serpentine) walls. Some block styles have prescored grooves so you can easily cut them into half-blocks with a hammer and masonry chisel or brickset for corner applications. Other systems include decorative cap blocks to finish off the top of the wall.

Interlocking blocks come in a range of sizes and shapes, but even the smallest weigh 40 to 60 pounds each. The standard size blocks weigh from 80 to 120 pounds each. Most have roughly textured faces created by cleaving off the front of each block after it's cast. Some shapes are designed especially for use in curved walls, but most will conform with curves easily. Most manufacturers provide a range of color choices, but styles and colors are limited by local supply.

Installing an interlocking block retaining wall

1 Remove sod from the wall project area with a sod kicker up to the top of the lawn slope **(See FIGURE A).** Plan for the top of the retaining wall to sit even with the top of the slope. *NOTE: If the slope behind the wall rises more than 3 ft., you'll need to terrace the hill with two or more retaining walls (See terracing illustration, page 57).* If you plan on re-laying the sod later, roll it up (green side in) and keep it moist.

2 Set up stakes and a leveled mason's line to mark the excavation area. The trench must be wide enough to include the width of the blocks plus 12 to 14 in. for installing backfill and drain pipe behind the wall. Using the mason's line as a guide, dig a flat trench deep enough to accommodate 6 in. of compactible gravel subbase plus ½ the thickness of the first course of blocks **(See FIGURE B).** Measure down from the string line to keep the bottom of the trench level. Once the trench is dug, remove the stakes and mason's line.

3 Fill the trench with 6 in. of compactible sub-base plus ½ in. to allow for compaction, then rake it smooth and compact it with a hand tamper **(See FIGURE C)**. The subbase serves as a footing beneath the block wall. Use a carpenter's level attached to a long, straight 2 × 4 to make sure the subbase remains level along the length of the trench.

HOW TO BUILD AN INTERLOCKING BLOCK WALL

FIGURE A: Remove sod from the project area up to the top of the hill slope, using a sod kicker or a square-nosed spade. If you plan to reuse the sod, roll it up and keep it moist.

FIGURE B: Mark the back of the excavation area with a mason's line and stakes. Dig a trench deep enough to contain 6 in. of subbase plus half the thickness of the first row of interlocking blocks.

FIGURE C: Fill the trench with 6½ in. of compactible gravel subbase and tamp it with a hand tamper. Check to be sure the subbase is level along the entire length.

FIGURE D: Set one block into the trench and mark its height with a leveled mason's line that runs the entire length of the wall. Lay the rest of the base course of blocks so their height aligns with the mason's line. Make adjustments to high blocks by tapping them with a rubber mallet.

4 Set a block into the trench at one end of the wall, then stake a mason's line so it is level and even with the top of the block, and runs the length of the wall. (The mason's line indicates the height of the first course of blocks.) Lay the first course (called the *base course*) into the trench, lining up the block faces, butting the front corners and making sure the block tops touch but do not move the mason's line. Add or remove subbase material beneath the blocks as needed to adjust their height. Check each block for level along the back edges and widthwise using a carpenter's level, and make fine adjustments by tapping the blocks with a rubber mallet **(See FIGURE D).** *NOTE: Some block manufacturers may suggest that you install the base course of blocks upside-down and backward, so that the flanged bottom edge of each block faces up along the front edge of the wall. This allows the block to rest flat on the subbase. Follow the manufacturer's instructions for proper block orientation on the base course.*

5 When you reach the end of the wall, cut a half block (widthwise) to fit into the corner, with the cut face facing frontwards **(See FIGURE E).** Then lay the base course of the end wall back into the hillside.

Cutting interlocking concrete blocks

Because most block walls are set in a running bond pattern, which results in staggered joints, you'll need to cut full blocks into half-blocks at wall ends and corners. Some manufacturers sell half blocks or right-angle corner blocks, but you can easily split full blocks in half with a brickset and hand maul. Some blocks have a shallow groove on the back face to make splitting easier. If the blocks you've purchased don't have these, use a circular saw equipped with a masonry blade to cut a 1/8-in.-deep groove along the top and back of the block. Then break the blocks by tapping along score lines. This will assure a clean, square cut, yielding usable left- and right-hand block sections.

6 Cut a length of landscape fabric wide enough to extend from the back edges of the blocks to the top of the excavation area, plus an extra 1 to 2 ft. that eventually will overlap and cover the rock backfill **(See FIGURE F).** Be sure that any seams between sheets of landscape fabric overlap by at least 6 to 8 in. The landscape fabric keeps soil from washing into the rock backfill material and potentially obstructing drainage.

7 Backfill the trench behind the blocks with a 3- to 4-in. layer of drainage rock to cover the landscape fabric in the trench bottom **(See FIGURE G).**

8 Designate one end of the trench to be the low end in order to establish a drainage slope that runs the full length of the wall. Water will pass from the surface of the hill down through the drainage rock backfill and into a perforated drain pipe that follows the trench. The pipe should lie on a slope that drops approximately 1 in. every 8 ft. to keep water from pooling behind the wall. Grade the drainage rock so it follows the proper slope to the low end of the trench, and lay flexible drain pipe (usually called *drain tile*) along the full length of the trench **(See FIGURE H).** Extend the pipe 1 or 2 ft. beyond the end of the wall or around it. This end should remain exposed and must be kept unobstructed

FIGURE E: Split a full-sized block in half to form the corner of the wall. The cut face should face forward.

FIGURE F: Spread landscape fabric into the trench so that it extends from the back of the blocks up the full height of the excavation. Allow 1 to 2 ft. extra along the top to fold back over the backfill material. If you need to use more than one continuous sheet of fabric, overlap the seams by at least 6 to 8 in.

FIGURE G: Backfill behind the base course of blocks with 3 to 4 in. of drainage rock, covering the landscape fabric on the bottom of the trench. Slope this rock layer 1 in. for every 8 ft. of wall length, down to the low side of the drainage trench.

FIGURE H: Lay perforated drain pipe (drain tile) in the trench. Extend the pipe 1 to 2 ft. beyond each end of the wall or wrap it around the wall so it faces the wall front. It will channel water away from the wall.

FIGURE I: Set the second course of block over the base course. The bottom back flange of each block should butt against the top back edge of the blocks below it. Stagger the joints from course to course.

FIGURE J: Cut and lay the corner blocks in the second course so they are staggered over the joints in the base course.

FIGURE K: Cover the drain pipe with drainage rock and continue backfilling in front of the landscape fabric and behind each additional course of blocks you lay. Tamp the backfill lightly with a hand tamper.

so runoff water can drain away.
NOTE: On long walls, you may have to lay additional courses of blocks at this stage and add more drainage rock backfill to establish the proper drainage slope for the drain pipe.

9 Lay the second course of block, butting the bottom flanges of the blocks tightly against the top back edges of the base course **(See FIGURE I)**. The pattern for laying block courses depends on the block design, but most interlocking blocks are laid in a running bond pattern, where each course offsets the course below it by ½ the block, creating staggered joints.

10 When you reach the end of the wall, place a full or partial corner block to form a staggered joint with the corner block beneath it **(See FIGURE J)**. Lay the second course for the side wall.

11 Backfill the trench with more rock, being careful not to dislodge the landscape fabric or disturb the drain pipe **(See FIGURE K)**. Fill the trench to a level about 2 in. below the top of the second course of blocks. Pack the rock backfill with a hand tamper.

12 Fold the extra landscape fabric over the rock backfill, then fill the rest of the trench up to the top of the second course of block with clean topsoil **(See FIGURE L)**.

13 Install the top course of blocks (called cap blocks) by adhering the cap blocks to the course beneath with a heavy bead of construction adhesive to hold them in place **(See FIGURE M)**.

14 Fill the rest of the trench in with clean, amended topsoil to a level 2 or 3 in. below the tops of the cap blocks **(See FIGURE N)**.

15 Patch over the excavation area with the sod **(See FIGURE O)** or fill the trench to the top with topsoil and use it as a garden bed for plantings.

FIGURE L: Fold over the extra landscape fabric to cover the drainage rock backfill, then fill the trench with topsoil up to the top of the second block course.

FIGURE M: Bond the top row of blocks to the course below with a heavy bead of construction adhesive.

FIGURE N: Fold the extra landscape fabric over the rock backfill and up against the backs of the cap blocks. Cover the fabric with topsoil to within 2 in. of the top of the wall.

FIGURE O: Patch over the excavation area with the sod. Press the sod firmly into the soil and water it daily for two weeks or until it establishes roots.

Before

This timber planting bed was built using the same basic techniques you'd use to build a timber retaining wall (See page 71). Positioned at the far end of the yard, it provides a pleasant barrier to street traffic visible from the patio at the opposite end of the yard.

Landscape Timbers

Back in the 1950s, railroad ties became a popular building material for raised planters, retaining walls, garden borders, patio edgings, steps, and the like. As railroad tracks were being torn up across the country in favor of freeways, air travel, and other modern forms of transportation, the recycled ties were readily available at lumber yards and building suppliers, at relatively low prices compared to other dimensional lumber of the same size. In recent years, however, railroad ties have become scarce, and now they're often quite expensive when you can find them. Because the ties are typically treated with highly toxic creosote, are often embedded with gravel, nails and tar (hard on saw blades), and come in limited lengths,

most professional landscape contractors prefer cleaner pressure-treated landscape timbers in their stead. Common sizes for landscape timbers are 5 × 6 in., 6 × 6 in., 6 × 8 in. and up, in various lengths. We used 5 × 6 timbers for this project.

Whether you use railroad ties or landscape timbers for your project, the concept is still the same: you can build a sturdy raised planting bed (information on building a timber retaining wall can be found on page 71) without the need for stakes to hold the timbers in place. Low retainers, freestanding walls and planters (up to 2 ft. in height) can be built easily by most do-it-yourselfers. For taller structures, seek the advice of a landscape architect or designer.

Building a raised planting bed with timbers

Calculate the amount of lumber you'll need for your planting bed by first creating a scale drawing of the planter on graph paper. For larger timbers, like those in our project planter, you'll save money if you try to design your planter to make maximum use of standard lumber lengths. It's also a good idea to stake out a full-size layout of your planter in the project area before you buy materials and start building to see how its size and shape will impact your yard.

1 Clear the planter project area of obstructions, then cut the first course of treated-wood timbers to size with a chain saw or circular saw and lay them out on the ground in the desired planter shape. *NOTE: If you choose to cut thick timbers with a circular saw, you may need to make a pass on two or more sides of each timber to cut all the way through.* Use a framing square to square up the corners **(See FIGURE A).** Butt the ends of these timbers in a consistent pattern around the planter perimeter so that the joints between courses of timbers do not align.

2 If you're installing the planter in a lawn area, cut the sod along the inside and outside edges of the loose-laid timbers with a square-nose spade to mark the locations of the timbers **(See FIGURE B).** If the planter will be installed over bare ground, mark the timber layout with spray paint or markers.

3 Set the timbers out of the way of the layout lines, then remove the sod within the layout lines with a square-nosed spade or a sod kicker **(See FIGURE C).** For our project planter, we used 5 × 6 treated timbers. For timbers this size, dig a trench where you've removed sod about 5 in. deep.

4 Fill the trench with 2½ in. of compactible subbase material and tamp it down with the end of one of the timbers **(See FIGURE D).** Level the subbase. The subbase layer provides a solid footing beneath the timber walls of the planter and promotes water drainage. The remaining trench depth will allow the first course of timbers to be about half below grade, which will help lock them into place and stabilize the base of the planter.

5 Before you permanently install the timbers for the base course, use a heavy-duty portable drill and spade bit to drill ½-in.-dia. guide holes through each timber **(See FIGURE E).** *NOTE: You may need to use a drill bit extension in order to drill through the timber in one pass.* For timbers up to 8 ft., drill a hole about 6 in. in from each end and one in the center. For timbers 10 ft. or longer, drill four evenly-spaced holes. Anchor rods will be driven through these holes later.

6 Place one of the longest timbers into the trench and check it for level. Add or remove subbase material as needed to level the timber and adjust its height **(See FIGURE F).** This leveled timber becomes a reference for leveling the other base course timbers.

HOW TO BUILD A RAISED PLANTING BED WITH TIMBERS

FIGURE A: Cut the base course of timbers and lay them into the project area to outline the planter's shape. Butt the ends of the timbers in a consistent orientation—each successive course of timbers should be staggered over the joints of the course below.

FIGURE B: Mark the outline of the timbers by cutting through the sod with a square-nosed spade.

FIGURE C: Set the base course timbers out of the way and remove sod from within the spaded outlines. Then dig a 5-in.-deep trench following the planter layout.

FIGURE D: Fill the trench with 2 to 3 in. of compactible gravel subbase to form a footing beneath the base course of timbers. Pack it down with the end of a timber and level the subbase layer all around.

Drill bit extension

FIGURE E: Drill three or four ½-in.-dia. holes in each base course timber, starting approximately 6 in. in from either end, to create guide holes for reinforcing rod anchors. Attach a drill bit extension to the end of your spade bit to bore through thick timbers.

FIGURE F: Set a long timber into the trench and level it by adding or removing subbase material beneath it. This timber will be a reference for leveling the other base course timbers.

FIGURE G: Set the remaining base course timbers into the trench and level each timber to the reference timber with a level and straight 2 × 4. Measure diagonally across the planter from the reference timber.

FIGURE H: Check each planter corner for square with a carpenter's square. Cut 18-in.-long reinforcing rod (rebar) anchors and drive them flush with the tops of the base course timbers, using a hand maul.

FIGURE I: Cut the second course of timbers to length, keeping in mind that the end joints should be staggered with those of the base course. Then lay the timbers in position.

7 Set the remaining base course timbers into the trench and butt the ends together to match the arrangement used in *Step 1*. Set a level on top of a straight 2 × 4 and lay it diagonally from the leveled timber across the base course in several directions to make sure all timbers are level to the long reference timber **(See FIGURE G).** Add or remove subbase material to level the rest of the timbers.

8 Cut 18-in. lengths of ½-in.-dia. reinforcing rod (rebar) with a hacksaw or reciprocating saw to serve as anchors for holding the base course of timbers in place. Use a framing square to check for square corners, then drive the rebar rods through the holes and into the ground with a hand maul **(See FIGURE H).** The tops of the rods should be flush with the tops of the base timbers.

9 Cut and lay the second course of timbers, overlapping the joints of the first course at each corner **(See FIGURE I).** As you install successive courses, you'll alternate the corner joints to form the lap pattern shown **(See FIGURE L for more corner detail).**

10 Attach the timbers at the joints, about 3 in. from the ends of each timber with 10-in. galvanized landscape spikes. Drill pilot holes for the spikes with a

bit extension and a ⁵⁄₁₆-in. spade bit, then drive the spikes into the timbers with a hand maul **(See FIGURE J).** Drive additional spikes 18 to 24 in. along the length of the timbers.

11 Drill ½-in. weep holes through the second course of timbers every 3 ft. around the planter. Start the holes midway up the width of each timber from inside the planter and bore outward at a downward angle. Aim for the exit hole to hit the joint between the two courses **(See FIGURE K).** *TIP: You could drill larger diameter weep holes and fit them with ½-in. PVC pipe "sleeves" glued in place with construction adhesive. Sleeves help prevent the wood around the weep holes from decaying.*

12 Cut and lay the remaining timber courses, overlapping the end joints and securing each course with landscape spikes **(See FIGURE L).**

13 Cut and attach full-width sheets of landscape fabric to the inside walls of the planter, with the top edges of the fabric positioned 2 to 3 in. below the top edges of the walls. The fabric forms a barrier to keep the soil inside the planter from seeping out between the timbers or clogging the weep holes. Staple the fabric in place with rows of ½-in. staples, spaced 8 to 10

FIGURE J: Attach the second course of timbers to the first with 10-in. galvanized landscape spikes driven through the timbers 2 or 3 in. in from the ends. Drill ⁵⁄₁₆-in. pilot holes to make the spikes easier to drive and to prevent splitting the timbers.

FIGURE K: Bore ½-in. weep holes through the second course of timbers, starting the holes from the inside of the planter, midway up the width of each timber. Drill downward and outward at an angle, aiming for the exit holes to hit the joints between courses.

FIGURE L: Cut and lay the remaining courses of timbers, securing each course to the one below it with landscape spikes. Be sure to overlap end joints so they interlock.

FIGURE M: Staple a sheet of landscape fabric around the inside of the planter, starting 2 to 3 in. below the top edges of the walls. Run extra fabric across the bottom of the planter.

FIGURE N: Add a 4-in. layer of drainage rock or compactible gravel subbase across the bottom of the planter to promote drainage.

in. apart **(See FIGURE M)**. Run excess fabric across the bottom of the planter.

14 Add a 4-in. layer of drainage rock or compactible gravel subbase across the bottom of the planter to promote drainage **(See FIGURE N)**.

15 Fill the planter with topsoil or planting mix **(See FIGURE O)**. Tamp the soil in 8-in.-deep layers with a hand tamper as you fill the planter to minimize settling once the planter is full. Otherwise you may need to add more soil seasonally. Finish the planter with water sealer or an exterior oil-based stain.

FIGURE O: Fill the planter with topsoil, tamping 8-in. layers as you go to help minimize further settling. Rake the top smooth.

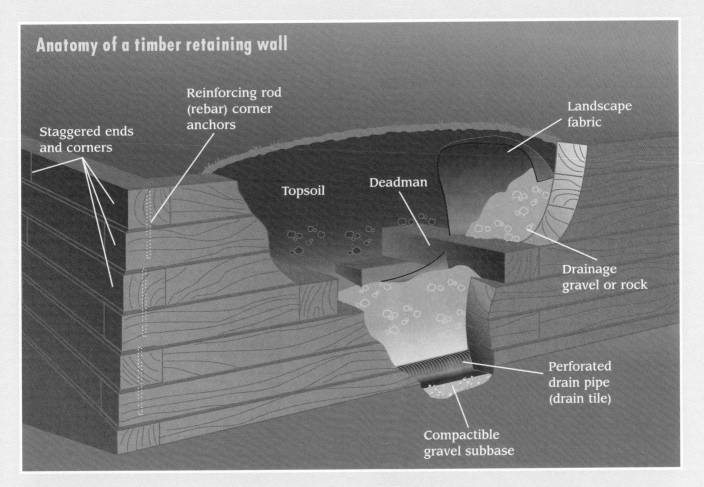

Anatomy of a timber retaining wall

Staggered ends and corners

Reinforcing rod (rebar) corner anchors

Topsoil

Deadman

Landscape fabric

Drainage gravel or rock

Perforated drain pipe (drain tile)

Compactible gravel subbase

VARIATION: Timber retaining wall

The information shown in the preceding project can easily be adapted to building a retaining wall from timbers. Timber retaining walls are less expensive to build than interlocking block walls but have a shorter life span and may look a bit "rustic" for many landscape designs. For walls up to 3 ft. high, use 5 × 6 or 6 × 6 pressure-treated timbers; taller walls may require larger-size timbers. Avoid using railroad ties as building materials, however, because they typically are soaked in creosote, which is harmful to vegetation.

Building basics

Foundation and drainage requirements are essentially the same as for interlocking block walls: The timber wall rests in a trench filled with a 6-in. layer of compactible gravel subbase, and the first course of timber sits half its thickness below grade. A perforated plastic drain pipe (drain tile) rests on the subbase and is set at a grade to facilitate water drainage. The wall is backfilled with river rock or coarse gravel. A layer of landscape fabric behind the rock backfill keeps soil from infiltrating the drainage materials.

The procedures for building timber retaining walls are similar to those for the raised planter on pages 66 to 70. The base-course timbers are anchored to the subbase with 18-in. lengths of ½-in. reinforcing rod, and 10-in. galvanized landscape spikes spaced every 2 ft. attach each course to the one beneath. Corner and end joints should be staggered. Set each course of timbers ½ in. behind the course beneath, so the wall forms a gradual backward angle (called "batter").

Reinforcing the wall

Timber retaining walls taller than 2 ft. require additional reinforcement. You have two basic reinforcement options: The most common is to install "deadmen" which consist of 3-ft.-long timbers extending horizontally from the face of the wall back into the slope, and attached to crosspieces of the same material with spikes (see the above illustration). Place the deadmen midway up the wall, spaced 4 to 6 ft. apart.

If there isn't enough space behind the wall to install deadmen, you can reinforce the wall from the front side by installing vertical anchor posts, cut from the same material used to build the wall. Space anchor posts 4 ft. apart, and set them below grade to a depth that equals ½ the height of the finished wall. It's a good practice to sink the bottoms of the posts in concrete. Stack the wall timbers flat against the backs of the anchor posts so the front face of the wall appears flush, rather than angling backward in batters.

Fences & Gates

Fences serve many purposes in your yard. They define boundaries, provide security and privacy, contain children and pets, serve as a windbreak, provide a backdrop or support for plantings, and more. Compared to solid masonry walls, fences are relatively easy and inexpensive to build. While installation can be done by one person, it's far easier if you enlist the aid of a helper.

Before you decide on a particular fence design or its location, check local building codes, city ordinances, and neighborhood covenants. These will dictate fence height, setbacks from property lines (or the street), and even the materials you can use to build the fence. For example, in residential areas, backyard boundary fences are typically limited to 6 feet; front yard fences, 3 to 4 feet in height. If you're building a boundary fence between your yard and your neighbor's you'll need to establish the exact location of the property line. Realize that you can't always rely on existing fences or other structures, or even on measuring the property yourself. If you have any questions as to where the property line is, hire a surveyor to establish it precisely. Also, it helps to discuss your plans with your neighbors (and ideally, enlist their help) to circumvent any future hard feelings or disputes regarding the fence. If in doubt, it's best to set the fence back at least 6 in. to 1 ft. from the property line.

Like any building project, building fence and gates requires requires careful construction work. But the fact is, most types of fences are much simpler to make than many other outdoor carpentry projects. The real key to a fence and gate project is in choosing the materials and style that best fit into your landscape. To get you started on the right foot, we've included a number of photos of successful fence and gate building projects in this chapter. Once you've selected a design and built your new fence, you'll find that of all the landscape building projects, adding fences and gates has perhaps the highest payback for the lowest investment of time and money.

Combine fence materials to create a unique fence that blends with your house style and follows the contours of your yard. Here, premilled fence pickets are attached to a framework of posts, stringers and skirt boards to manage a gentle slope in the yard with a fence that retains a consistent height throughout.

Prefabricated fence panels are suspended between fence posts to create a tall privacy fence that has the appearance of requiring much more work than actually went into it. Prefabricated panels are generally sold in 8 ft. lengths, in a range of styles, heights and materials (See page 75).

Stick-built fences can share design elements with prefabricated fence panels, but at the same time they offer greater flexibility. Because they're assembled on-site, one board at a time, they can be adapted easily to short runs (it's much easier to cut two stringers to length than to try and cut whole fence panels to length). And if your height requirements are non-standard (as with the 52-in.-high fence shown here), it's much easier to cut fence boards before attaching them than to trim panels and remove and relocate the lower stringer.

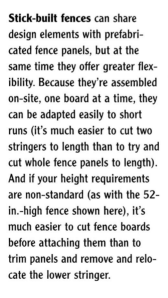

Pickets are often scalloped between fence posts to create a sense of flow and Country-style charm.

Tall privacy fences create a feeling of intimacy and have an added benefit as windbreaks.

Overhead structures, such as arbors and pergolas, enhance the character of fences and gates when the style and materials are complementary.

A decorative top treatment can transform a bulky, stockade-type fence into a landscape highlight.

A matching gate can be built simply by cutting down the same style prefabricated panels used for the fence. Try to plan the gate so you have at least a half-picket at each end. A diagonal cross-brace should be installed between the stringers on panels clad only one side.

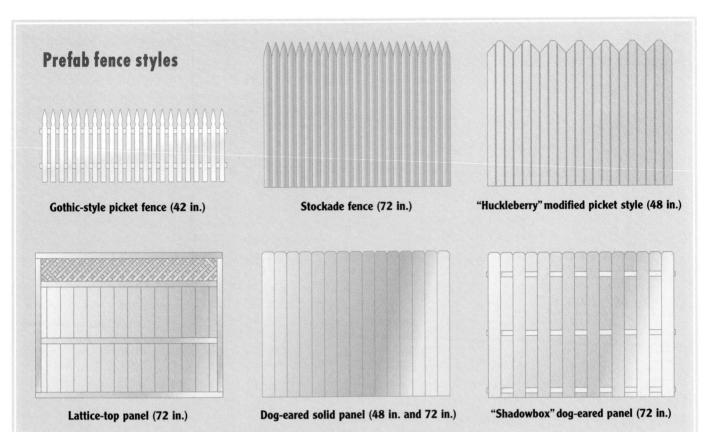

Prefab fence styles

Gothic-style picket fence (42 in.)

Stockade fence (72 in.)

"Huckleberry" modified picket style (48 in.)

Lattice-top panel (72 in.)

Dog-eared solid panel (48 in. and 72 in.)

"Shadowbox" dog-eared panel (72 in.)

A sampling of the most common prefabricated fence panels sold at building centers today. Most can be purchased in cedar or pressure-treated pine. If you can't find the style or size you're looking for, inquire at the lumber counter about custom-ordering fence panels.

Shadow-box style prefabricated fence panels are popular because they add privacy and wind-screening without the drawbacks of solid panels.

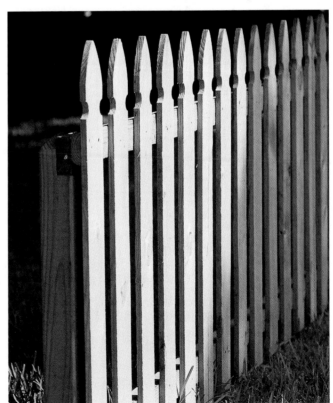

Classic picket fences can be purchased as prefabricated panels. There are many options for size, spacing and the shape of the picket finial.

Anatomy of a Fence

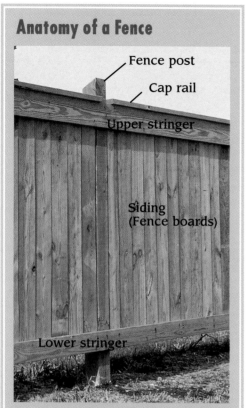

Fence post

Cap rail

Upper stringer

Siding
(Fence boards)

Lower stringer

Fences consist of posts that support at least two horizontal stringers. Generally, the posts are not more than 8 ft. apart. The fence boards, called the "siding," are attached to the stringers. Some fences include top treatments, such as a cap rail or lattice top, or post caps and finials

Setback distance

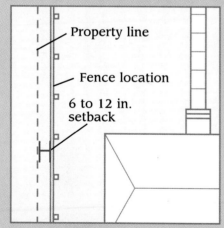

Property line

Fence location

6 to 12 in.
setback

Build fences at least 6 to 12 inches on your side of property lines. The buffer helps ensure that the structure is completely on your property, in the event the property line is not accurate or you veer away from the line during construction. If your fence or part of your fence is found to be on your neighbor's property, you may be ordered to remove and relocate the fence.

Post caps and finials give fence posts a decorative touch, and also protect the end grain of the posts from direct exposure to the elements. Choose caps or finials (or a combination of the two) that blend with the style and proportion of your fence and gate.

Fence Basics

The three basic components of a fence are posts, stringers (also called *rails*), and siding (the fence boards). Optional components include a cap rail, post caps or finials, and skirtboards between the bottom of the fence and the ground. When we think of fence siding materials, wood boards or pickets immediately come to mind, although a variety of other materials are commonly used, such as plywood, ornamental iron, steel, aluminum, chain link, welded wire, and vinyl plastics. All-vinyl fences have become a popular alternative to wood and imitate many popular wood designs, such as vertical board, picket, post-and-rail, lattice, and so on. These are often sold in kit form, which includes posts, prefabricated panels, and all the hardware/fasteners necessary to assemble them.

The framework. Typically, the framework of a fence consists of 4 × 4 posts and 2 × 4 top and bottom rails (either laid flat or on edge) to which you attach the siding (boards, pickets, plywood, wire, etc.). Although the posts and rails can be of redwood, cedar, or other naturally decay-resistant species, pressure-treated lumber is often used for these components, as it is typically less expensive. Even with pressure-treated wood, it's a good idea to treat all cut ends with a wood preservative, especially those that come in contact with the ground.

Attaching the stringers. Nailing or screwing the stringers to the posts provides a relatively weak attachment. Fence panel hangers (See page 78) will hold up better and are easy to use. For best results, cut dadoes into the posts for the stringers: Before setting the posts, lay them on a flat surface and mark the width and depth of the dadoes with a pencil and square. The dadoes should be no more than ½ in. deep, or they will weaken the post. When marking the dado locations, always measure down from the top of the post. After marking all posts, use a circular saw to make a series of ½-in.-deep saw cuts within the cutout area, then remove the waste with a hammer and wood chisel.

Gate hardware

Hardware required to install and operate gates includes hinges and a handle or handle/latch assembly. You may want to add closer hardware for gates that get heavy use. Because gates receive a lot of abuse, use the largest hinges that will fit your fence and gate framework, while still keeping within the aesthetics of the overall fence and gate design. Tall gates (5 ft. or taller) often employ a third hinge installed midway between the top and bottom hinges. Commonly, the screws supplied with prepackaged gate hinges and latches are too short to adequately secure them for heavy repeated use. So, substitute longer screws (of the same type) that extend at least ¾ the way into the gate posts and frame. See pages 86 to 87.

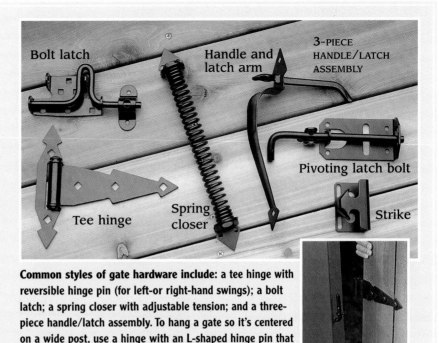

Common styles of gate hardware include: a tee hinge with reversible hinge pin (for left-or right-hand swings); a bolt latch; a spring closer with adjustable tension; and a three-piece handle/latch assembly. To hang a gate so it's centered on a wide post, use a hinge with an L-shaped hinge pin that mounts directly into the post (inset photo).

Applying wood preservative

Fences and gates (and any outdoor structure made from wood) will last longer if you apply a clear preservative, water repellent wood conditioner to all surfaces. Although these products provide some protection against decay, the primary reason for using them is to "stabilize" the wood to help prevent initial warping and splitting of fence boards and rails, due to changes in temperature and humidity. They also protect against ultraviolet (UV) radiation to keep wood looking "new" longer. However, these products will not keep the wood surface from weathering over time. CAUTION: Many wood preservatives are toxic; wear heavy gloves, goggles, long-sleeve shirt and a cartridge-type respirator (designed to filter mists and vapor) when applying these products. Read label precautions.

Finishing options for fences and gates include: staining with an exterior wood stain (often redwood); priming and painting; or clear-coating with clear wood sealer. If using pressure treated lumber, look for sealer designed for this material.

If you favor the look of a weathered fence, you can speed up the process and achieve an evenly weathered surface by applying a wood bleach. If not, your other options are to paint or stain the fence.

Stains are easier to apply than paint, especially on rough boards, but they will require more frequent reapplication to maintain their appearance. Most top-quality "preservative-stains" contain a water repellent, UV inhibitors, and a mildew-cide, thus they can be applied directly to bare wood without need of a clear sealer/preservative. If using paint, make sure it contains mildew-cide. If you've already applied a wood preservative or water repellent, or if you've used green (unseasoned) redwood or cedar, wait at least 3 months before painting or staining the fence.

OPTIONS FOR ATTACHING STRINGERS TO POSTS

Light
duty

Medium
duty

Heavy
duty

After your posts are set, attach stringers (sometimes called rails) between the posts to support the fence siding. The quickest and cheapest method is simply to toe-nail the stringers to the posts with 8d galvanized common nails (left photo). But use this method only for very lightweight siding or fill material, such as lattice panels. For prefabricated fence panels, attach metal fence hangers (middle photo) to the posts, then fasten the stringers in the hanger hardware. For heavy siding and fences that are exposed to high wind, cut dadoes into the posts for the stringers (right photo).

TOOLS FOR BUILDING & INSTALLING FENCES & GATES

Tools you'll need to build and install fences and gates include: (A) power miter saw; (B) circular saw; (C) posthole digger; (D) spade; (E) 4-ft. level; (F) post level; (G) mason's line; (H) framing square; (I) tape measure; (J) reciprocating saw; (K) jig saw; (L) drill/driver; (M) pencil; (N) hammer; (O) speed square.

Before

Stick-built fences

Unlike fences made with prefabricated fence panels, stick-built fences are created board-by-board at the building site. There are many good reasons why you may choose to stick-build your new fence rather than building it with panels: If your yard is sloped or hilly, you can adjust the length of each individual fence board to follow the terrain, while maintaining a level line on top. If your planned fence line is irregular or contains numerous short jogs, trying to cut full panels to length and fit them between posts can be very tricky. If you have a particular building material, size or fence style in mind, you can stick-build the exact fence you want. But another reason to stick-build your fence should not be to save money. If you calculate the per-foot cost of prefab panels versus the materials needed to make your own fence, you'll find that the panels usually come out cheaper. But the trade-off is that with panels, you don't have the ability to select each piece of stock, and you can easily end up with lower-grade building materials.

A

FIGURE A: Mark the borders of the fence with wood stakes and mason's line. Be sure the corners of the fence layout are square.

Building a wood fence

As shown, this project fence design employs 6-ft.-long posts set 5 ft. above ground, to support a shadowbox fence with a fence board height of 52 in.

Plotting the fence

1 Stake out the fence layout by driving stakes at the end or corner post locations, then stretching a mason's line between the stakes. Use a line level to level the line. At fence corner locations, square the corner string lines by using the "3-4-5" triangulation method. Measure off 3 ft. along one string line from the corner stake and 4 ft. off the adjacent string line from the stake. The lines are square to one another when a 5 ft. tape measure line intersects the 3- and 4-ft. string markings. Adjust the stakes and strings accordingly until the fence corners are square.

2 Locate the centers of intermediate posts by measuring along the string line in 6- to 8-ft. equal intervals. Use a plumb bob to transfer the post locations from the string to the ground. Mark the locations with stakes **(See FIGURE A).** *NOTE: When figuring the spans between posts, it's important to consider the width of the vertical fence boards you'll use, the spac-*

Options for digging postholes

Posthole digger

Gas-powered auger

EASY AUGER

If you have only a few post holes to dig, and the required hole depth does not exceed 30 in., use a hand-operated clamshell-type posthole digger (left). For deeper holes, or if you have a lot of holes to dig, rent a gas-powered auger (above) from a tool rental shop. Gas-powered augers come in one- and two-person models and save a considerable amount of time and labor. The model shown here uses the weight of the motor as a counterbalance to help withdraw the auger from the hole.

ing you plan to leave between the fence boards (at least ⅛ in.), and their arrangement on the stringers between the fence posts. Plan this now; otherwise you may have to rip-cut the width of one or more vertical fence boards later to get the fence board arrangement to fit between the posts. Once you've determined post locations, remove the strings.

Installing the posts

3 Dig the post holes, removing each stake as you go (See *TIP,* previous page). Check local building codes for required post depth in your area. This will determine the length of the posts you'll need to buy. As a general rule, plan to set about ⅓ of the total post length into the ground. Another guideline is to sink posts 2 ft. deep for a 5-ft.-tall fence; 2½ ft. for a 6-ft.-tall fence; and 3½ ft. for an 8-ft.-tall fence. The diameter of the hole should be about twice the diameter of the post. Make the post holes slightly larger at the bottom than at the top to form a bell shape that helps anchor the posts when you fill the hole with concrete.

4 Fill each post hole with 5 to 6 in. of compactible gravel subbase to provide drainage beneath the posts **(See FIGURE B).** Tamp it down with the end of a post or hand tamper.

5 Set one of the end or corner posts first. Lower the post into the hole and use a post level or two carpenter's levels held on adjacent sides of the post to plumb the post vertically. Be sure the overall above-ground length of the post is a few inches longer than planned finished height of the post. (The posts will get trimmed to final height later.) Attach temporary braces to the post on two adjacent sides to keep the post plumb while pouring the concrete footing **(See FIGURE C).** Each brace consists a 2 × 4 about 4 ft. long and tacked with a single pivot nail or screw to a stake that is driven in the ground. With the post held plumb, attach the top ends of both braces to the post with 3-in. deck screws.

6 Loosely set and brace the post at the opposite end of the fence line in the same manner as *Step 3,* keeping the overall above-ground height of the posts equal. Attach a leveled line between the posts. To do this, measure down a precise distance from both post tops (for example, 1 ft.) and mark reference lines. Tack or screw small spacer blocks of equal thickness to the same side of both posts, then attach mason's line to the blocks, aligning the line with the marks on the posts. (The spacer blocks will keep intermediate posts from throwing the string line out of alignment when you set the posts). Adjust the height of one of the end posts until the string line is level and remove or add gravel subbase as needed beneath this post to estab-

FIGURE B: Fill each post hole with 5 to 6 in. of compactible gravel subbase and tamp it down. The subbase will help water drain away from the post bottoms.

Post level

FIGURE C: Plumb end posts with a post level and brace them into position with 2 × 4 braces screwed to the posts and staked into the ground.

FIGURE D: Set intermediate posts with braces and stakes, using a scrap 2 × 4 spacer board between posts. Then fill the post holes with concrete.

FIGURE E: Snap a leveled chalk line along all the posts to mark cutting lines for trimming the posts to final height.

FIGURE F: Extend the chalk lines on the posts to all four faces with a pencil and trim the posts with a circular or reciprocating saw.

lish its new height. This top string line will serve as a reference for keeping intermediate post heights approximately the same as the two end or corner posts.

7 Attach a second leveled string line 8 to 10 in. up from ground level. Use spacers behind this string line as well (they should match the thickness of the spacers used for the top string line). These two string lines serve as reference lines to help keep the faces of intermediate posts lined up with one another. Plumb and brace intermediate posts and use a loose spacer to check the distance between each post and the string lines. We cut a piece of 2 × 4 to serve as a temporary spacer between posts to keep the distance between all posts uniform. Once the posts are in position, recheck to make sure the fence line is straight.

8 Fill each post hole with premixed concrete **(See FIGURE D)**. Add just enough water to the concrete to form a stiff consistency. Overfill the holes 1 to 2 in. above ground level, then use a short wood block or masons trowel to slope the surface away from each post on all sides (called crowning) in order to direct water away from the posts. Before the concrete sets up, make sure the posts are still plumb and lined up. Readjust the braces, if necessary. Then remove the two string lines, but leave the post braces on until the concrete has fully cured (about two days).

9 Attach a level chalk line to the two end posts to mark post height **(See FIGURE E)**. Snap a line onto all posts at once. Scribe pencil lines around all four sides of each post at the chalk line and trim the posts to height with a circular saw or reciprocating saw **(See FIGURE F)**. *NOTE: 4 × 4 posts, like those shown here, are thicker than the maximum cutting depth of most circular saws, and must be cut in two passes from opposite sides of the post. Getting the cuts to line up can be tricky, so take your time.*

Adding stringers

10 Establish the locations of two stringer boards between the fence posts by measuring down from the post tops. On taller fences or fences with heavy siding, you'll need to add a center stringer to support the weight of the fence boards. In installations where stringers are made from dimensional 2× material, like 2 × 4s, and fit between each two posts, attach the stringers with galvanized 2-in. metal fence brackets **(See FIGURE G)**. We centered our brackets on the inside faces of the posts and attached the brackets with 2-in. deck screws.

11 Measure and cut the stringers to length **(See FIGURE H)**. *NOTE: It's a good idea to measure*

FIGURE G: Mark the stringer heights on the posts. Attach galvanized metal fence brackets at these locations, using 2-in. deck screws.

FIGURE H: Measure the distance between fence posts to determine the length of the stringers. Measure and cut the stringers to length.

all the spans between the posts first, even if you're confident that the distances are the same. This way, you won't gang-cut all the stringers only to find that some are too short. Cut stringers ¼ in. shorter than the span distance so they'll slip easily between the fence brackets.

12 Coat the cut ends of all the stringers with wood preservative to protect them from absorbing moisture and rotting **(See FIGURE I).**

13 Set the top and bottom stringers into the fence brackets and attach them with 1½-in. galvanized deck screws **(See FIGURE J).**

Modifying fence sections

14 The path of the fence shown here was interrupted by a large tree—a frequent problem encountered when installing fences. We decided to attach the fence to the tree rather than rerouting the fence. In these situations, build a modified fence section to fit the profile of the tree trunk from 2 × 2 dimension lumber. Attach it to the closest fence post with galvanized deck screws **(See FIGURE K).**

15 Drill a ⅞-in. hole through the bottom stringer of this fence section and drive a piece of galvanized pipe down through the stringer hole and into the ground **(See FIGURE L).** The pipe acts as a bottom brace for the fence section and is easier to install than digging another full-depth post hole this close to tree roots. It also is less damaging to the tree roots.

16 Anchor the top of the fence section to the tree by screwing an eyebolt into the tree trunk.

FIGURE I: Coat the ends of the stringers with wood sealer to keep them from absorbing moisture and eventually rotting.

FIGURE J: Set the stringers onto the fence hangers and secure them with 1½-in. galvanized deck screws.

FIGURE K: Modify short lengths of fencing as needed to fit against obstructions like trees. Support these sections with temporary wood spacers and screw the framework to the closest fence post.

FIGURE L: In locations where full post depth is not possible, drive a length of ¾-in. galvanized pipe through the stringer and into the ground.

Connect the fence section to the eyebolt with several lengths of heavy, braided wire cable threaded through the fence framing and a turnbuckle. Tighten the turnbuckle until the fence section doesn't wobble—but not so tight that it pulls the fence section away from the metal fence brackets **(See FIGURE M).** After the fence is built, check support cables periodically to make sure they're taut. Tighten the turnbuckle if there is too much play in the cables.

Attaching fence boards

17 Determine the length of your vertical fence boards and cut them to size. If you have a power miter saw, you can cut the boards quickly and easily by setting up a stop block on your work surface to index off each fence board at the correct cutoff length **(See FIGURE N).** Typically, the bottoms of the fence boards should be at least 2 in. above ground level to prevent contact with the ground, which can cause the boards to rot. The tops of the fence boards should not extend more than 6 in. above the top stringer, or they may warp.

18 Starting at one end post, plumb the first fence board and attach it to the stringers with 1½-in. galvanized nails or screws (use two fasteners per stringer). It's important that the first board be attached so that it is perfectly plumb—it becomes a reference board for all boards down the line. If it isn't plumb, the rest of the fence boards will be off, and the inaccuracy will get progressively worse as you go.

19 Attach the rest of the fence boards, checking frequently for proper alignment and plumb **(See FIGURE O).** A pneumatic nail gun makes quick work of attaching fence boards, but galvanized screws work equally well and make removing fence boards easy should some need replacement in the future. In the project shown here, we used one of the fence boards (painted white in the photo) as a spacer for establishing the *shadowbox* fence board pattern. If the boards in your design will butt against one another on the same side of the stringer, leave a ⅛-in. gap between them (8d nails serve as handy spacers).

20 Apply a finish to the fence (See page 77). We used oil-based, redwood-tinted stain, applied with an air-compressor-driven spray gun **(See FIGURE P).** Wear a respirator when spraying on a finish. Build and install a gate after the fence is complete (See pages 86 to 87).

FIGURE M: Attach fencing to trees by screwing a large eyebolt into the tree trunk. Secure the frame to the tree with cable and a turnbuckle.

FIGURE N: Cut fence boards to length. A power miter saw and a stop block allow you to gang-cut fence boards quickly and accurately.

FIGURE O: Set a mason's line as a reference to establish location for the tops of the fence boards, and attach the boards to the stringers with nails or screws, aligning the top of each board with the mason's line. Use a spacer board, where possible, to keep fence board spacing even.

FIGURE P: We used a compressor-driven spray gun to apply oil-based stain to this fence. Always wear a respirator when applying a sprayed finish.

FIGURE A: Measure the distance between the two gate posts and subtract 1½ in. for clearance to determine the actual width of the gate.

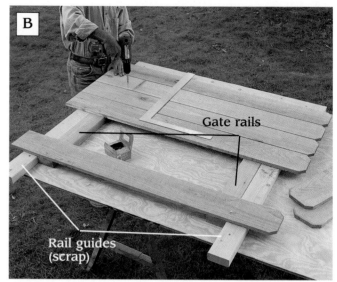

FIGURE B: Attach fence boards to the gate rails with screws. Scrap rail guides screwed in place keep the gate rails parallel during assembly.

FIGURE C: Measure and cut a diagonal cross brace to fit between the gate rails and screw the fence boards to it.

FIGURE D: Lay out and cut any decorative profiles in the top of the gate, being careful not to cut through the gate rail frame.

Gates

As with fences, there are many methods for building a gate. The one we constructed for our project fence is a typical residential gate, which consists of a simple 2 × 4 frame with diagonal bracing covered with fence boards that match the fence.

1 Measure the distance between the inside faces of the gate posts on either side of the gateway (See FIGURE A). Subtract 1½ in. from this measurement to determine the actual width of the gate (which leaves ¾ in. of clear space on either side of the gate). The gate opening should be at least 36 in. wide to accommodate lawn and garden equipment or two people passing through at once. The width between the posts should not vary by more than ¼ in., top to bottom. Gate height will differ, depending upon the height of the fence, but

plan for the gate to hang at least 2 in. above ground.

2 Cut the gate frame rails and fence board siding to length and lay the gate framing members on a flat surface, fence board side facing up (See FIGURE B). Typically the top and bottom rails of the gate frame will align with the fence stringers. Screw the fence boards to the rails with 1½-in. galvanized deck screws, keeping each fence board perpendicular to the gate rails. Use two screws per joint. *TIP: To keep the gate rails parallel during this step, screw scrap-wood rail guides to your work surface, spaced so that the gate rails fit between them.*

3 Flip the gate over so the gate rails face up, and check the gate for square by measuring the diagonals. Select a length of stock for a gate cross brace that is longer than the diagonal distance between the gate

FIGURE E: Mark hinge positions on the gate and attach hinge leaves, screwing them through the fence boards and into the gate rails.

FIGURE F: Prop the gate into position, attach hinge hook hardware to the gate post and hang the gate.

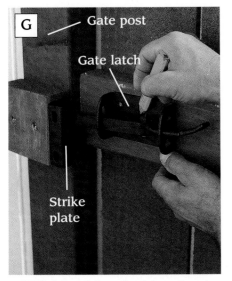

FIGURE G: Install the strike plate on the gate post, align the latch and mark drilling locations.

FIGURE H: Bore holes through the gate rail for thumb latch hardware with a spade bit.

FIGURE I: Install the thumb latch and handle to the outside of the gate with screws.

rails. Lay it on top of the rails so it intersects the inside opposite corners of the rails. Mark the cutting angles so the cross brace will fit between the rails **(See FIGURE C).** Cut the cross brace to length and screw the fence board siding to it with 1½-in. deck screws.

4 Mark and cut any decorative profiles in the top of the gate with a jig saw **(See FIGURE D).** We chose a scallop that begins and ends one fence board in from either edge of the gate. Then stain or paint the gate to match the fence.

5 Measure and attach tee-hinge leaves to the gate, screwing them through the fence board siding and into the gate rails **(See FIGURE E).**

6 Prop the gate in the gateway with wood support blocks placed under the bottom rail. Provide at least

2 in. of clearance between the bottom of the gate and the ground. Measure and attach hinge hardware to the hinge-side gatepost and hang the gate **(See FIGURE F).** Test to make sure the gate swings freely and make any necessary adjustments before installing the latch.

7 Install the strike plate on the gatepost. Position the latch assembly on the upper gate rail, align it with the strike plate and mark pilot and latchbore hole locations on the gate rail **(See FIGURE G).**

8 Bore holes for thumb latch hardware with a spade bit, according to the manufacturer's instructions **(See FIGURE H).** Attach the latch to the gate.

9 Install the handle and thumb latch assembly to the outside of the gate **(See FIGURE I).** Test the operation of the latch mechanism and adjust as necessary.

Prefabricated fence panels

Prefabricated fencing comes in a variety of styles to suit many landscape designs (See page 75). The picket fence shown here is built with Gothic-style, 42-in.-high by 8-ft.-long fence panels.

1 Plot the fence line and set the posts as described on pages 80 to 82, locating the postholes so facing edges of adjoining posts will be 8 ft. apart (if using 8-ft. long panels). At this point, it's a good idea to take actual measurements of the panels—they can vary slightly from the stated length, and you'll want to space your posts to reflect any variation. Lay out your gate locations at this time as well. Plumb and brace the posts and set them in concrete.

2 Mark top and bottom stringer locations for each full-length fence section on the fence posts, and attach metal fence hangers to the posts with 2-in. galvanized deck screws. For this fence, we centered the fence brackets on the inside faces of each post. Set full-length fence sections onto the fence hangers and fasten them with 1½-in. deck screws **(See FIGURE A).**

3 Mark fence sections that will need to be cut to fit shorter spans between posts, measuring the distance between the inside faces of the posts **(See FIGURE B).** Plan these cuts where possible so that they fall on stringers rather than down the length of fence boards, and try to keep the spacing consistent between posts and the fence boards on either side. Attach fence

hangers to these posts, and fasten the stringers of the cut panels to the hangers with deck screws.

4 We decided to modify a length of the prefab fencing for use as a gate in our project fence. The gatepost spacing on either side of the sidewalk required us to cut the gate to size by ripping the end fence boards. In cases like this, set the gate section into position and use the gate posts as references to mark cutting lines **(See FIGURE C).** Subtract an additional ¾ in. from each side to provide clear space between the gate and the posts. Lay out the gate so you'll cut the fence boards to even widths on both sides.

5 Cut a diagonal cross brace to fit between the two stringers and screw it to the stringers with 3-in. deck screws **(See FIGURE D).** Strengthen the gate frame by screwing the pickets to the cross brace with 1½-in. deck screws (use two screws per joint).

6 Sand the gate and fence members as needed with a palm sander using medium-grit sandpaper **(See FIGURE E).** Attach the gate to the fence posts with hinges, and install latch hardware (See pages 86 to 87 for more information on installing gates).

7 Seal the fence with several coats of oil-based primer and paint, stain, or water sealant **(See FIGURE F).** It's a good idea to cover sidewalks, grass and plants to protect them from drips or overspray, especially if you spray on the finish.

FIGURE A: Set posts, then attach full-length fence sections between the posts with metal fence hangers and galvanized deck screws.

FIGURE B: Mark cutting lines for fence sections that will need to be shortened using the fence post on each side as references.

FIGURE C: Set the gate section into place and mark the gatepost locations onto the panel. Subtract ¾ in. from each side to allow for clear swinging space and cut the gate to size.

FIGURE D: Measure and cut a cross brace to fit between the gate stringers and attach the cross brace to the stringers and fence boards with galvanized deck screws.

FIGURE E: Sand out rough spots or splinters from the gate and fence with a palm sander and medium-grit sandpaper. Hang the gate.

FIGURE F: Seal all wooden fence surfaces with primer and paint, stain or wood sealer. Be sure to wear safety glasses and a respirator if you decide to spray your fence.

Building Decks

A maze of stairs, platforms, planters and benches gives this richly finished deck an appealing, mysterious quality.

Building Decks

Only a generation or two ago, wood decks were a seldom-seen curiosity in the backyards of American homes. But today, in just about every type of neighborhood across the entire country, you're likely to find an abundance of decks sprawling out from patio doors or stepping gracefully down the hilly terrain. The reason for the explosion in popularity is twofold: as suburban housing developments have sprung up outside the crowded cities, the average yard size has increased dramatically; and, as leisure time has increased, we've come to focus our search for family relaxation first and foremost in our own backyards.

Building a simple wood deck is not difficult or expensive. In essence, it is only a raised wooden plat-form supported by posts set in concrete. For many homeowners, a plain, square deck is more than adequate to meet their relaxation and entertainment needs. But if you aspire to creating an outdoor living area that is truly unique and has character, scale and function that go well beyond the ordinary, deckbuilding is an excellent vehicle for your pursuit.

On the following pages you'll find plenty of straight-forward information on how to build a deck. But we've taken the information a step further. If you've ever seen a stunning, elaborate deck that's rich with attractive features and wondered to yourself "How did they build that?," then you'll enjoy examining the following chapters: in them you'll find the answers.

Airy screens, wooden planters and strategically placed foliage create a private retreat that doesn't feel like a fortress.

Own your own island in the sun by building a freestanding platform deck in your favorite corner of your yard.

An ordinary entry area is transformed into a shaded resort by adding an L-shaped, multi-level deck with a handsome arbor.

New outdoor living space is carved out from a hillside with retaining walls and an expansive wood deck.

A built-in bench provides a resting spot for travelers seeking to ascend the steep slope that is home to this multi-level deck.

Tiered planters form a transition between this deck and the thickly wooded yard that surrounds it.

An outdoor room, complete with an arbor-and-trellis ceiling and built-in furniture, can be created with a little bit of imagination and an impeccable sense of design.

A stunning view becomes a work of art when framed by the strong lines of this deck and overhead arbor.

Interesting angles and subtle step-downs are the stand-out features in this beautiful and highly functional deck.

Deck Basics

Whether you're building a deck as a simple addition to your yard or as part of a more ambitious landscaping project, begin by learning the basics of deck design and deck anatomy, and work toward drawing detailed plans of your deck and building site.

Basic deck anatomy

Before you make your final working drawings, you'll need to identify all the various structural components that will make up your deck. A simple deck platform typically consists of the following elements: footings, posts, beams, joists, and deck boards. If you'll be attaching the deck to your house, you'll also need to attach a ledger board to your home to support the deck framing. For a finished appearance, you can also install fascia boards around the deck perimeter.

Footings: Concrete footings must be sturdy enough to support the entire weight of the deck plus any loads applied to it. You can take one of several approaches to make the footings. The type you choose depends on the type of soil you're dealing with, as well as the height and size of the structure itself. If you're building a low, freestanding deck on firm, stable, well-drained soil, the footing can consist of a precast pier block placed directly on the ground, or set in a shallow hole filled with poured concrete. The pier blocks have inset wooden tops, and sometimes metal post anchors to which you attach the posts. In firm soil, you can also simply dig a hole (typically 12 to 14 in. in diameter) to the desired depth and insert a metal connector or post anchor into the wet concrete. The holes for these footings should be wider at the bottom than at the top to create a "bell shape" for greater stability. In very loose soil (such as sand or gravel), ready-made concrete tube forms are used to keep the sidewalls of the hole from collapsing into the space to be occupied by the poured concrete. In all cases, the bottom of the footing should extend below the frost line, and the top should be at least 3 in. above finished grade.

Posts: These usually are made from 4 × 4s or 6 × 6s, set on-end on top of the footings. They serve to transfer the weight of the deck to the footings beneath. If the deck will be 4 ft. or more above ground level, the posts may require cross-bracing.

Beams: These members provide the main horizontal support for the deck. One common type of beam consists of two 2 × 8s or 2 × 10s fastened to opposite sides of the posts with through-bolts or lag screws, or set into notches cut into the beams. Another common practice is to attach solid 4 × 6 or 4 × 8 beams to the tops of leveled posts with metal connectors. For low-level decks, you can attach the beams directly to leveled pier blocks or footings, eliminating the posts entirely.

Ledger boards: If the deck is attached to the side of the house, the wall of the house must support one end of the deck. In this case, you'll need to install a ledger board to which you attach the joists. The joists may either rest on top of the ledger or be hung flush against the face of the ledger. The method of attaching the ledger to the house depends on the type of house siding you're dealing with.

Joists: These typically consist of 2 × 6s or 2 × 8s attached to the beams to support the decking. Depending on your design requirements, the joists can either run across the tops of the beams, or be hung between them with joist hangers. On attached decks, the joists typically run perpendicular to the house wall, attached to the ledger at one end, with a 2 × 6 or larger header joist at the other end. Bridging or blocking installed between the joists may be required.

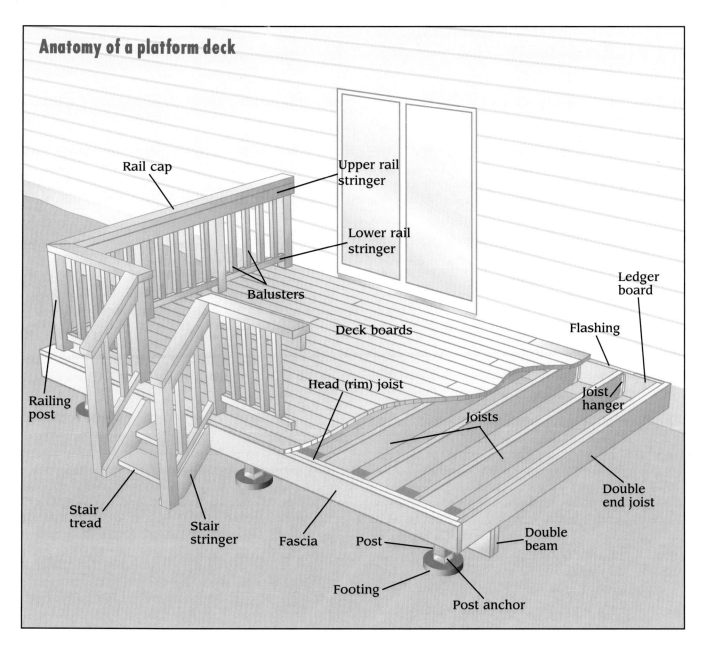

Anatomy of a platform deck

Rail cap

Upper rail stringer

Lower rail stringer

Balusters

Deck boards

Ledger board

Flashing

Railing post

Head (rim) joist

Joists

Joist hanger

Stair tread

Stair stringer

Fascia

Post

Footing

Post anchor

Double beam

Double end joist

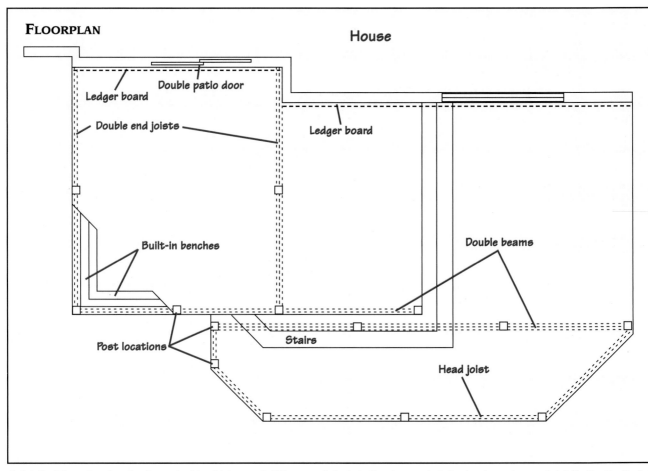

FLOORPLAN

House

Ledger board

Double patio door

Double end joists

Ledger board

Built-in benches

Double beams

Post locations

Stairs

Head joist

A detailed floorplan drawing is required to obtain your building permit. Include the above-noted structural members and details. For the final plan drawing, also indicate joists and joist spacing (24 in. on-center is suitable for most decks), overall dimensions and joinery plans.

Decking: The deck surface can be built with 2 ×4s or 2 × 6s (actual thickness is 1½ in.) laid flat across the joists and fastened to the joists with galvanized deck screws. Wider boards generally aren't used because they have a greater tendency to cup and split over a period of time. You can also use premilled deck boards, which are thinner (1¼ in. thick) but are usually cut from select lumber and feature rounded "bullnose" edges, rather than the sharp edges found on dimension lumber. Most deck boards are a nominal 6 in. wide (5¼ in. actual width). Because the decking is the most visible part of the structure, you'll want to choose the lumber carefully. For the sake of appearance, most professional designers and builders prefer to use natural redwood or cedar for decking, as well as for the other visible components, such as steps, railings, benches, and the like. Pressure-treated lumber is frequently used for the structural components (posts, beams, joists), but can be used for the decking as well if cost is the main concern. For more on choosing lumber, see page 102. To add visual interest, you can lay the decking in a variety of patterns (herringbone, diamond, or basketweave, for example—see pages 104 to 105). Because the decking pattern can influence the spacing

and location of joists, plan the substructure to provide support where deck boards meet.

Fascia Boards: Primarily a decorative element, fascia boards are often attached to the ends of the deck (and sometimes the sides) to cover the exposed ends of the deck boards. Made of the same material as the decking, fascia usually looks best if the bottom edge is flush with, or extends slightly below the bottoms of the end joists and headers. On low-level decks, make sure the bottom edges of fascia boards are at least 3 in. above ground level.

Drawing plans

Drawing deck plans is done in stages as your ideas and construction details are finalized. Your initial design plan should show the size and location of the deck in relationship to the house and other major features on the property. Use the drawing as a base for developing working drawings that detail the framework, joinery and decking pattern, then create final scaled "blueprints" that feature an overhead floorplan and an elevation drawing, along with materials lists and estimated costs (you'll need all of this information to obtain a building permit for your project).

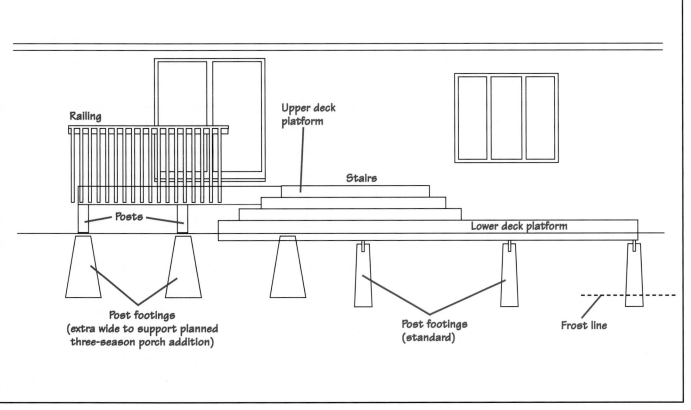

Railing

Upper deck platform

Stairs

Posts

Lower deck platform

Post footings
(extra wide to support planned
three-season porch addition)

Post footings
(standard)

Frost line

An elevation drawing should indicate the height and size of the various deck components, including the post footings. In addition to the above-noted elements, include dimensions, height above grade and indicate structural joinery methods.

For most deckbuilding projects, you should invest some time and money up front consulting with a professional designer or architect. Their input can actually save money in the long run, and will help ensure that you get results you're happy with from all your hard work. You should also contact your local building inspector early in the process. He or she will review your preliminary plans to suggest improvements and to identify any additional information you'll need to obtain your permit when your finished plans are ready for presentation.

Spans and Spacings

The spans and spacings between the various deck members—posts, beams, joists and decking—are determined by the size, lumber grade and wood species of these components, as well as the type of decking used, and the decking pattern. When planning spans and spacings, start from the top down by choosing the size and pattern of the decking first. Then, determine the joist spacing (for example, 16 or 24 in. on-center). Next, determine the span between beams, based on joist size and spacing. Then determine the post span based on the distance between joists. Finally, choose

Recommended spans & spacing

MAXIMUM DISTANCE BETWEEN JOIST SUPPORTS:

	Joist spacing (o.c.)		
Joist size	12"	16"	24"
2 × 6	11' 7"	9' 9"	7' 11"
2 × 8	15' 0"	12' 10"	10' 6"
2 × 10	19' 6"	16' 5"	13' 4"

MAXIMUM DISTANCE BETWEEN POSTS SUPPORTING BEAMS:

	Joist span			
Beam size	6'	8'	10'	12'
4 × 6	8'	7'	6'	5'
4 × 8	10'	9'	8'	7'
4 × 10	12'	11'	10'	9'
4 × 12	14'	13'	12'	11'

RECOMMENDED POST SIZE:

	Load area*				
Deck height	48	72	96	120	124
0' to 6'	4 × 4	4 × 4	6 × 6	6 × 6	6 × 6
6' and up	6 × 6	6 × 6	6 × 6	6 × 6	6 × 6

*To calculate "Load area" multiply the distance between the beams by the distance between the posts (in feet).

Designing for deck height

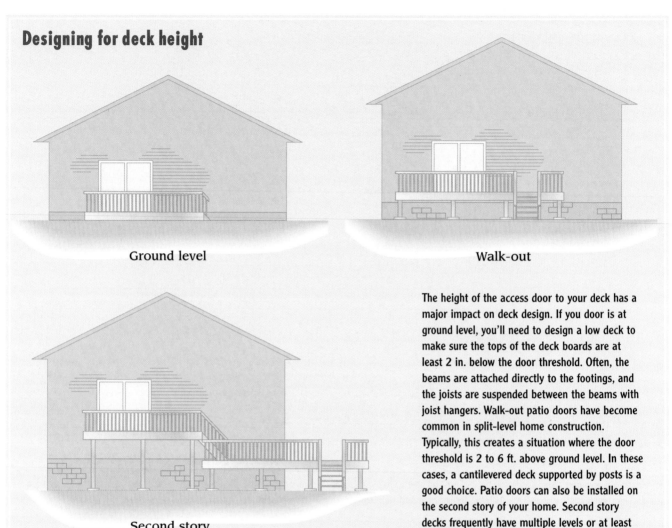

Ground level

Walk-out

Second story

The height of the access door to your deck has a major impact on deck design. If you door is at ground level, you'll need to design a low deck to make sure the tops of the deck boards are at least 2 in. below the door threshold. Often, the beams are attached directly to the footings, and the joists are suspended between the beams with joist hangers. Walk-out patio doors have become common in split-level home construction. Typically, this creates a situation where the door threshold is 2 to 6 ft. above ground level. In these cases, a cantilevered deck supported by posts is a good choice. Patio doors can also be installed on the second story of your home. Second story decks frequently have multiple levels or at least wide landing areas to eliminate long staircases.

the post size, which should be determined by the deck height and load area. Use the table on the previous page as a general design guide, but be sure to double-check your figures with local code requirements and have your plans approved before building the deck.

Bear in mind that designing the deck with larger-size components (2 × 8 joists and doubled 2 × 10 beams, for example) will enable you to increase spans and spacings, thus requiring fewer beams, posts, and footings, which can save you time and money. However, this will also raise the minimum height to which you can build the deck, which may or may not coincide with your plans.

The spans and spacings of these various components will determine the post and footing locations on the site, which must be indicated on your plan drawings. Many professionals prefer to cantilever the deck structure several feet beyond the supporting posts, to hide unsightly footings and piers. As a general rule, you can cantilever beams and joists a distance equal to ⅓ their allowable spans between supporting members.

For example, a beam with a 9-ft. span can be cantilevered up to 3 ft. beyond the perimeter post. A joist with a 6-ft. span can be cantilevered 2 ft. beyond the end beam. Check local codes. If you want to cantilever the deck, locate the footings accordingly.

Multi-level decks. Decks with multiple deck platforms are more complex to design and build than single-level decks, especially when it comes to framing and support. In some cases, it's possible to use the same structural network to support more than one deck platform. But frequently, the platforms are designed and built as independent structures, then connected via stairs, railings or single-step stepdowns.

Stairs, railings & other features

Be sure to include detailed drawings of stairs, railings and other deck features, like built-in benches or planters, in your drawings. If you're building a multi-level deck, include drawings for the transition between levels. See the chapters on these features for more design information.

Hand tools used in deck construction include: (A) speed square; (B) mason's line; (C) framing square; (D) hand saw; (E) aviator snips; (F) caulk gun; (G) 4 ft. carpenter's level; (H) combination square; (I) spirit level; (J) pencil; (K) line level; (L) 50 ft. roll tape; (M) rigid tape measure; (N) chalkline; (O) wood chisels; (P) utility knife; (Q) socket wrench; (R) hammer; (S) flat pry bar; (T) hand maul; (U) plumb bob.

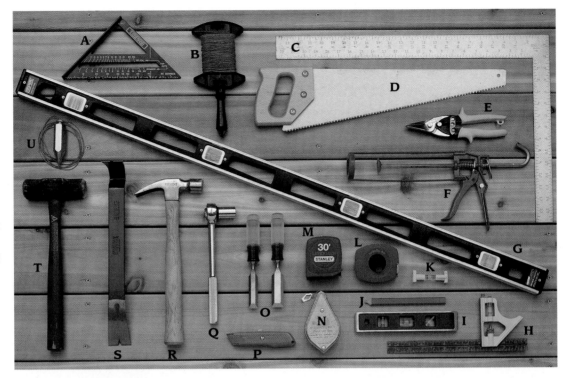

Power tools you'll need to tackle a deck-building project may include: (A) power miter saw; (B) portable table saw; (C) circular saw (preferably a worm-drive saw); (D) cordless drill/driver with replaceable battery pack; (E) ½ in. corded drill; (F) reciprocating saw.

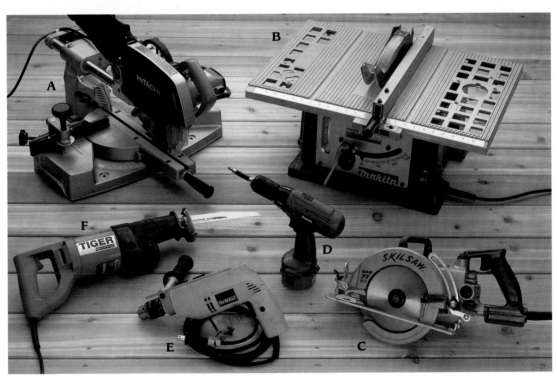

Tools & materials for building decks

Using quality materials and the right tool for the job will make your deckbuilding project run smoothly. In addition to obtaining the tools shown in the photos above, you may want to look into renting a gas-powered auger for drilling post holes. A compressor-driven nail gun is a big help when attaching decking.

The photos on the following pages show the various fastening devices and metal connectors used to join

deck components. All fasteners and connectors should be galvanized to resist rust and be specified for exterior use. While metal connectors aren't absolutely necessary for assembling a deck, they provide a much stronger connection than nails or screws alone. Using the appropriate connectors to reinforce joints will extend deck life considerably, so it's well worth the relatively small amount of extra money you'll pay for these items.

Tips on buying lumber

When you go to buy lumber and other materials, make up an estimate sheet with columns for the sizes, lengths and quantity needed for the various structural components (posts, beams, joists, ledger, decking, etc.), as well as required hardware, concrete and other miscellaneous materials. For each item, add 5% to 10% extra to allow for waste, lumber defects, and building errors. If possible, hand-pick all lumber at the yard, even if you plan on having it delivered at a later time.

Take your list to several local outlets and do a bit of comparative shopping. Traditional lumberyards usually offer the widest variety of lumber sizes, lengths, and grades, and have knowledgeable personnel who can help you estimate the amount of materials you need. Large home centers and self-serve building emporiums generally sell lumber at cheaper prices, but have a limited selection of sizes and grades. However, these outlets often run sales, in which you can buy part of your lumber and other materials at a good discount.

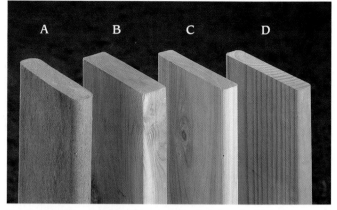

Decking options include: (A) composite deck boards; (B) 2 × 6 or 2 × 4 dimensional lumber; (C) 1¼ × 6 in. premilled cedar or redwood deck boards; (D) pressure-treated deck boards.

Masonry-related materials for footings include: (A) concrete tube forms (8 in. and 12 in. dia. shown); (B) pre-mixed concrete; (C) precast concrete piers (alternative to pouring footings).

Deck boards can be attached to the joists with 10d galvanized nails, but for more strength, use 3-in. deck screws. Some builders like to provide further reinforcement by laying a thick bead of construction adhesive along the tops of the joists before attaching the boards.

Fasteners:

• *J-bolts* (also called L-shaped anchor bolts) with nuts and washers are used to attach post anchors to concrete footings. These are installed while the concrete is still wet.

• *Lag screws and washers* are used to join larger deck components, such as 2× beams to the sides of posts, railing posts to the sides of the deck, as well as

certain types of hardware, such as metal stair cleats. They're often used in conjunction with lead lag screw shields to attach ledgers to masonry walls or concrete foundations.

• *Hex-head machine bolts, nuts and washers* have some of the same applications as lag screws (such as attaching double 2 × 10 beams to the sides of posts) but provide a stronger connection.

• *Galvanized nails* of various sizes provide the least expensive means of assembling deck components, but also make the weakest connection. Common nails have more holding power than box nails but are more likely to split the wood at board ends. Galvanized finish nails are used to attach decorative trims and moldings, where nail heads would be unsightly. These are usually countersunk with a nailset, and the holes filled with exterior spackle or wood putty.

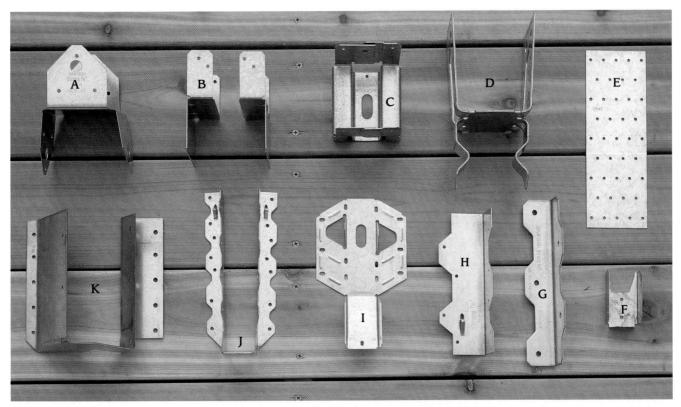

Galvanized metal connectors include: (A) one-piece post cap (4 × 4); two-piece adjustable post cap: (C) stand-off post anchor; (D) post anchor with concrete fins; (E) tie plate; (F) fence hanger; (G) staircase angle bracket; (H) right-angle connector; (I) skewable joist hanger; (J) joist hanger; (K) angled joist hanger.

• *Galvanized deck screws* (also called *all-purpose* or *bugle-head* screws) have perhaps the widest variety of applications in deck construction, and provide a stronger connection than nails. Coarse, aggressive threads and a bugle-head design enable you to power-drive the screws flush to the wood surface without the need of predrilling pilot holes, as you would for conventional wood screws. Don't confuse these with non-galvanized black drywall screws, which are meant for interior uses only.

Galvanized Metal Connectors:

• *Post anchors* are attached to concrete footings to hold the deck posts in place and to elevate the post base to help prevent moisture from wicking into the end grain.

• *Joist hangers* are used to attach joists to the ledger and head joist. On low-level decks, they're used between beams. Variations include angled joist hangers and double joist hangers. Similar hangers are available for 4× lumber. Special 1¼ in. joist nails are used to fasten the hangers.

• *Angle brackets* help reinforce inside corners, such as where a head joist meets an outside joist. Heavier angle irons may be used to reinforce post-to-beam connections.

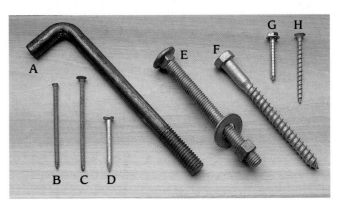

Fasteners for deck construction include: (A) J-bolt; (B) galvanized finish nail; (C) coated sinker; (D) joist-hanger nail; (E) carriage bolt with nut and washer; (F) lag screw; (G) hex-head screw; (H) deck screw.

• *T-straps and metal cleats* are used to reinforce post-to-beam attachments, as well as for butt splicing joists and beams.

Flashings: Galvanized sheet metal or aluminum flashing is used in conjunction with caulk to protect the ledger board, house siding, and the ends of deck boards from water damage. Preformed flashings of various sizes and shapes are available at hardware stores, lumberyards and home centers. If none of the preformed flashings fits your particular situation, you can make your own from flat stock, by bending it into the shape needed.

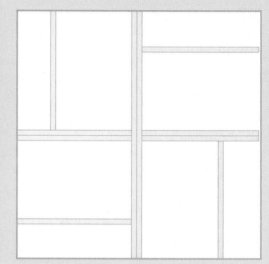

Basketweave pattern, sometimes called "parquet" pattern.

Herringbone pattern (sometimes called simply "diagonal pattern" if only one row of end joints is used).

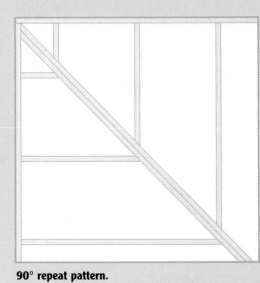

90° repeat pattern.

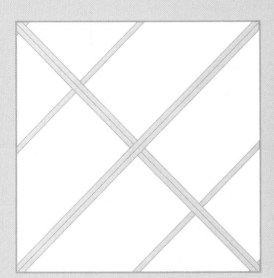

Concentric repeating mitered squares.

Deckbuilding: An overview

1 **Create the layout** (pages 108 to 112)
2 **Pour the footings** (pages 113 to 117)
3 **Attach the ledger** (pages 118 to 121)
4 **Install posts & beams** (pages 122 to 131)
5 **Install joists** (pages 132 to 133)
6 **Attach deck boards** (pages 136 to 137)
7 **Build stair frame** (pages 138 to 143)
8 **Add treads & remaining deck boards** (pages 144 to 145)
9 **Build railings** (pages 146 to 153)
10 **Apply finishing touches** (pages 156 to 157)

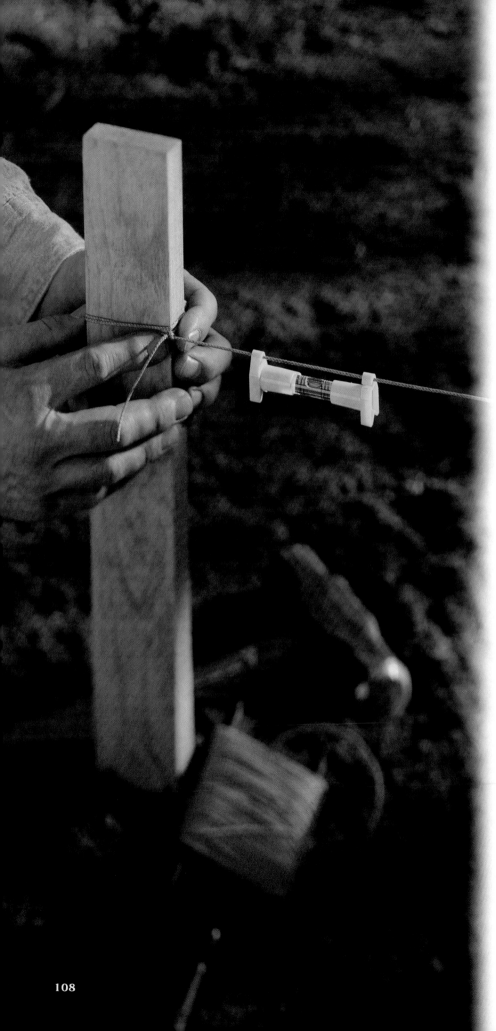

Deck layout

Careful layout work is the cornerstone of a successful deckbuilding project. If the corners are square and the footings are level and in the right spots, you'll enjoy the benefits throughout the entire construction process. But if the key structural members of the deck are misaligned, you'll spend the rest of the project trying to recover.

The conventional method for laying out a deck is to use batter boards and mason's lines to outline the project area and to establish position for the footings that will support your deck posts.

Before you start laying out your deck, check to see that the site has adequate drainage. Make sure the ground slopes away from the house (at least 1 in. per 8 ft.), and that there are no low areas that will collect water. Also make sure any runoff from roof gutters is directed away from the deck site. To do this, you may need to connect the downspout to a perforated drain pipe, placed in a gravel-filled trench that leads to a dry well on a lower part of the property. Also remove any sod, weeds, dead roots, wood scraps, or other organic matter from the site. Do not treat the soil with pesticides, weed killers, or other chemicals at this time. If desired, you can apply these later, after the substructure is built and you're ready to lay down the decking.

Provide a space convenient to the site for storing lumber and other materials. Stack the lumber neatly on scraps of wood to keep it off the ground. Do all the preparatory or organizational work you can do prior to setting your layout lines. Less activity around the lines once they're set decreases the probability that they'll be accidentally knocked out of alignment.

Creating the deck layout

The first phase of deck construction is to establish layout strings and batterboards to locate the footings for the deck posts. For decks attached to the house, first mark the ledger board location on the house wall and use this as a reference point to establish layout string lines for determining footing locations. Refer to your deck plan drawings for specific ledger details and post spacing.

1 Use a pencil, tape measure and level to mark a ledger board outline on the house wall **(See FIGURE A)**. Mark the end of the ledger with a dotted line (normally, ledger boards are the same width as the deck joists). Mark another dotted line that represents the outside face of the end joist. If you'll be attaching a fascia board to the outside of the end joist (forming a double end joist), also mark its outside edge.

2 Measure in from the dotted line that indicates the end of the ledger and make a second reference mark to indicate the centerpoints of the posts that will be installed inside the end joist **(See FIGURE B)**. Drive a nail at this post mark on the bottom edge of the ledger outline. It will serve as a tie-off point for the mason's line.

3 Erect a batterboard about 2 ft. beyond the corner post location, determined by your deck plan drawings. Use a tape measure squared to the house with a carpenter's square to find the approximate spot **(See FIGURE C)**. *NOTE: Batterboards consist of pairs of scrap wood stakes connected to a wood crosspiece with deck screws. The batterboards should be tall enough so that they can be driven into the ground about 8 to 12 in.—their purpose is to hold layout strings taut.* Size the batterboards so that when they're driven into the ground, the top edge of the crosspiece will be roughly level with the bottom edge of the ledger board.

4 Run a mason's line from the nail you tacked on the house wall at the ledger site to the batterboard and pull it

HOW TO CREATE THE DECK LAYOUT

FIGURE A: Draw the outline of your ledger board on the side of the house, noting locations for end joists and fascia boards with dotted lines. Be sure the ledger outline is level.

FIGURE B: Mark the ledger outline as a reference for locating the corner posts. Drive a nail at this mark to serve as a layout line tie-off.

FIGURE C: Install a batterboard about 2 ft. beyond the corner post location so the crosspiece is roughly even with the nail you drove into the ledger outline.

FIGURE D: Tie off a mason's line to the nail in the ledger and run the line over the top of the batterboard crosspiece. Pull the line taut.

FIGURE E: Use the 3-4-5 triangulation method to square the layout line to the house. Adjust the line back and forth along the batterboard crosspiece until a 5-ft. section of the tape measure intersects both the 3- and 4-ft. index marks. This ensures that the line is square to the house. Drive a nail into the batterboard and tie off the string at this spot.

taut **(See FIGURE D).** With a helper, square the line to the house wall, using the "3-4-5" triangulation method. Establish the triangle as follows: Measure out 4 ft. along the string from the house wall and mark this spot with masking tape. Next, measure 3 ft. from the string at the ledger outline and make a second mark. Use a tape measure set at 5 ft. to measure diagonally between the two reference marks you've just made. Adjust the string back and forth on the batterboard until the distance between the other two reference marks is exactly 5 ft. **(See FIGURE E).** Drive a nail into the batterboard crosspiece to mark where the string crosses it, and tie off the string. The layout line is now square to the house.

5 Level the layout line established in *Step 4*, using a line level **(See FIGURE F).** Raise or lower the batterboard as necessary to make minor leveling adjustments.

Mark post locations

6 From the house wall, measure along the layout line and mark the line with masking tape at the middle of the corner post **(See FIGURE G).** To find the point, refer to the plan drawings for your deck and find the distance from the outside front face of the corner post to the house. Subtract half the thickness of the post from this distance (remember to use actual dimensions, not nominal), and mark your string line at that point. Repeat the batterboard squaring process to set a second layout line at the other end of the ledger, parallel with the first layout line. You've now established two of the three deck platform dimensions.

7 Position a second set of batterboards perpendicular to and approximately 2 ft. outside of the first two layout lines. The corner post marks on the first two strings should roughly align with the crosspieces of the new batterboards **(See FIGURE H).** Run a third layout line between these two batterboards so it intersects the corner post marks on the original two layout strings. Pull the line taut and tie it off to nails driven into the batterboard crosspieces. Level the third layout line by adjusting the batterboards.

FIGURE F: Suspend a line level from the layout line and adjust the batterboard up or down as needed until the layout line is level.

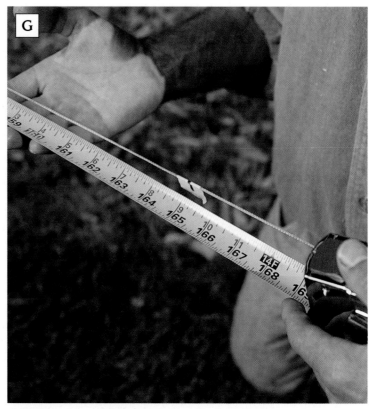

FIGURE G: Measure out from the house along the layout line to determine the center of the corner post. Mark the centerpoint with masking tape.

FIGURE H: Erect two more batterboards 2 ft. outside of and perpendicular to the first two layout lines. Run a third layout line between these batterboards so it crosses the corner post tape marks on the original layout lines.

FIGURE I: Check the layout for square by measuring diagonally from the ends of the ledger outline to both string intersection points. The layout is square when the diagonals are equal. Adjust the string lines if necessary.

FIGURE J: Mark the front layout line for additional post locations, using masking tape.

FIGURE K: Drop a plumb bob down from the post marks on the layout lines to mark the post locations on the ground. Drive a stake at each post location.

FIGURE L: Set up additional batterboards and layout lines to mark post locations for your entire deck. Once the batterboards and strings are removed, the stakes will serve as references for digging post holes.

The intersecting strings should just touch one another where they cross. Their intersection points mark the center of the corner posts.

8 Use a tape measure to check the length of both diagonals between the string intersection points and the ledger ends **(See FIGURE I).** Adjust the strings as necessary so both diagonal measurements are exactly the same, assuring a perfectly square deck layout.

9 Measure in from the layout string intersection points to locate the centerpoints of intermediate posts that will be positioned along the head joist of the deck. Use masking tape to mark post locations on the front layout line **(See FIGURE J).**

Stake the footing locations

10 Drop a plumb bob down from each masking-tape mark to establish the centerpoints of the posts on the ground. Drive a wood stake into the ground at each of these locations **(See FIGURE K).** These stakes serve as markers for digging and installing the tubular footings that will support the posts.

11 Since our multi-level project deck has two platforms, and each platform is larger than could be supported by a ledger and corner posts alone, we needed to install additional posts in the center areas of each deck platform. To pinpoint the centers of those posts, we tied off mason's line to layout strings already in place. We also erected more batterboard sets and ran string lines to establish our second, lower deck platform elevation **(See FIGURE L).** Regardless of the complexity of the deck you plan to build, keep all layout lines for each deck platform uniformly square and leveled at the appropriate height. This way, you'll ensure that footings for the posts will line up properly with deck framing members.

12 Make sure you've accounted for all post locations outlined in your deck plan. It's more difficult to determine post locations once you've taken down the layout strings. Remove the strings, but leave the batterboards in place.

Footings

After you've located and marked the footing positions on the deck site, the next step is to dig holes at the marks, and pour the concrete deck footings. Depending on your soil conditions, you may need to use a form to contain the concrete and keep the walls of the hole from collapsing. In the project featured here, we use tubular concrete forms to build the footings. The tubes come in various diameters and have a wax coating on the inside to keep the concrete from bonding to the form.

When your building department inspects your deck project, the footings are generally their primary area of interest. They'll check the depth to make sure the footings extend below the frost line (if applicable to your area of the country), and they'll check the diameter to make sure the footing is strong enough to support your deck. Contact your inspector to have him review your project after the footing holes are dug, but before you pour the concrete.

If you're only pouring a few shallow footings, it's easiest and cheapest to mix your own concrete on site. But if you'll need more than ½ cubic yard (about 14 cubic feet), look into having ready-mix concrete trucked in to your site (but don't schedule delivery until your footing holes and layout have been approved). Since each 60-pound bag of premixed concrete yields only ½ cubic foot of material, you'll need to mix upwards of 30 bags by hand just to create ½ yard. To put the numbers into perspective, if you're using a 12-in.-dia. tubular form, each 60-pound bag of premixed concrete will fill up about 9 in. of the form.

Before the concrete cures, you'll need to embed a device in the concrete for anchoring the deck posts. One option is to insert a metal J-bolt in the center of each footing, with the threaded end up. Or, you can install post anchors with preattached corrugated fins that are submerged into the concrete while it's still wet. In the project shown here, we use the J-bolt method, primarily because it's easier to control the height and position of the posts when using J-bolts.

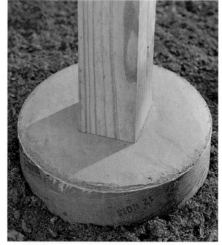

Set a J-bolt into the freshly poured concrete footing, centered with the threaded end sticking up. After the concrete cures, insert metal post anchor hardware over the J-bolt and thread a washer and nut to secure the anchor to the J-bolt.

Set posts directly into concrete. This is a little risky—if you manage to keep the post immobilized as the concrete sets up, you can end up with an almost-indestructible bond. But if the post slips, gaps are created and a loose fit (and water penetration) can result.

Post anchors with preattached corrugated fins can be inserted directly into the fresh concrete. Do your best to level the post anchors as you insert them. Do not disturb the anchors until the concrete has cured.

Footing options

In addition to the conventional method of pouring subterranean footings and embedding hardware into the fresh concrete, you may have other options for making deck footings.

Precast concrete piers. This method is commonly used in mild climates with stable soil. When frost lines are not an issue, you can simply pour shallow concrete footings, then set precast concrete piers on top of the footings after they cure. At the footing locations, dig 12-in.-deep holes (or as required by local codes) that are 3 in. wider in dimension than the base of the pier block (pier blocks are normally 12 × 12 in.). Tamp loose soil in the bottom of the hole, then shovel in a 2-in. layer of coarse gravel and tamp firmly. Pour concrete into the holes, filling them to within 3 to 4 in. of ground level. While the concrete is still plastic, but strong enough to support the pier, embed the pier about 1 in. deep into the concrete footing. Use a plumb bob to align the center of the pier block with the post centers marked on the guide strings. The top of the pier block should be level and at least 3 in. above ground. After the concrete cures, simply set 4 × 4 posts on-end into the recess at the top of each pier.

Above-ground tube footings. You can extend tubular forms one or more feet above grade to double as posts or columns to support the deck beams (common on hillside decks). If the tubes extend 2 ft. or more above the ground, you'll need to brace them with 1 × 4 or 2 × 4 braces as you would for a fence post. Insert a No. 5 reinforcing rod (rebar) into the footing after you've poured in the concrete, to prevent it from cracking. Because you'll be attaching the beams directly to the poured-concrete columns with metal connectors, you'll also need to make sure the tops of the form tubes are level to each other. Do this by attaching a string between the tops of the tubes, then leveling the string with a line level; or you can place a long, straight 2 × 4 on-edge across the tops of the tubes, and set a carpenter's level on top of the 2 × 4. Make any minor height adjustments when you install the tubes. Also run leveled strings out from the bottom of the ledger, centered over the post locations. Position the strings above the tubes to indicate the width of the beam, then measure down from the string to the tops of the tubular forms to indicate the beam width plus ½ in. Set the tubes to this height.

NOTICE: **Before you locate footings, make sure you know the exact locations of any underground electrical, gas, telephone, sewer and water lines within the deck area. Utility companies can provide you with this information; some offer a free locating service. Also check the original plot plans for your house, if you have them.**

Installing concrete tube footings

1 Dig post footings at each stake location to the appropriate depth (below frost line), as specified in building codes for your area. Dig each footing 3 to 4 in. deeper to allow for a drainage layer of compactible gravel subbase at the bottom. Depending upon the size and depth of your footings, as well as the number of holes you'll need to dig, it may be well worth the money to rent a one- or two-person gas-powered auger to excavate your footings **(See FIGURE A).** For holes shallower than 35 in., you could also use a post-hole digger.

2 Remove any loose soil from the bottom of each hole with a post-hole digger. Use a story pole to check the depth of the holes **(See FIGURE B)** and remove more soil, if necessary. The hole depth should be uniform for all footings. Add 3 to 4 in. of compactible gravel subbase, and tamp the bottom of each footing hole with a hand tamper or 4 × 4 scrap.

3 Measure the hole depth again, add 3 in., and cut the concrete tube forms to length with a hand saw or reciprocating saw. Make sure you cut the tubes evenly all around so the tube tops remain flat. Set the tubes into the footing holes **(See FIGURE C).** Each tube rim

FIGURE A: Dig post footings to the depth specified by building codes in your area. For large decks with many footings, rent a two-person gas-powered auger to excavate the holes.

Story pole depth marker

FIGURE B: Clear away any remaining loose soil from the bottom of each footing hole and check the depth with a story pole marked with a line at the proper depth. Add 3 in. of compactible gravel subbase and tamp this drainage layer down.

FIGURE C: Cut the concrete tube forms to length (depth plus 3 in.) and set them into the holes. Each tube should extend 3 in. above grade. Then backfill around the outside of each tube with soil and level the tops.

FIGURE D: Transport ready-mix concrete to posthole locations in a wheelbarrow. Lay a path of boards across your yard to make carting the cement easier and to protect your yard.

FIGURE E: Dump wheelbarrow loads of concrete into the tubular forms until they're nearly full to the top.

should extend 3 in. above ground level, which will keep the deck posts from absorbing ground moisture and rotting. Backfill around the tubes with soil, keeping each tube level. Then tamp the backfill.

4 For smaller decks with only a few footings, consider buying bags of premixed concrete for filling footings and prepare it in small batches yourself. On larger deck projects with multiple footings, have ready-mix concrete delivered to your site. If you must transport wet concrete a distance from the truck, use wide boards to make a path for the wheelbarrow **(See FIGURE D).** A path will spare your yard from wheel ruts and spillage and it also makes rolling the wheelbarrow easier.

5 Dump wet concrete from the wheelbarrow into each tube and fill it nearly full **(See FIGURE E).** If you have many footings to fill and a concrete truck waiting at the curb, time will be of the essence, so work carefully but quickly. Have a helper guide the concrete into the tube with a shovel as you pour. If some concrete does land outside the tube, don't shovel it back in, as it will be contaminated with dirt, which will weaken the footing as the concrete cures.

6 Top off each tube by shoveling in wet concrete until it overfills the tube **(See FIGURE F).**

7 Plunge a long length of scrap wood into the wet concrete, moving it up and down around the tube to settle the concrete and remove air pockets **(See FIGURE G).** If the concrete settles below the tube rim, refill it so it crowns the top of the tube.

8 Use a length of 2 × 4 to screed off the wet concrete level with the top of the tube **(See FIGURE H).**

9 Replace the layout lines between the batterboards and the house and re-level them, if necessary. Center a J-bolt over each tube, using a plumb bob dropped from the string lines. Insert the J-bolt into the wet concrete (hook end first), wiggling it slightly as you submerge it to remove any air bubbles **(See FIGURE I).** Leave about 1 in. of the bolt protruding above the concrete. Check the bolt with a try square to make sure it is perfectly vertical. Wipe any wet concrete off the J-bolt threads before it cures.

10 Allow the concrete to fully cure (about three days in dry weather). At this point in the deck construction process, you can remove the batterboards.

FIGURE F: Use a shovel to finish filling the tubular forms with concrete. Overfill the forms slightly.

FIGURE G: Plunge a length of scrap wood into the wet concrete and work it up and down to settle the concrete and remove air pockets.

Create a clean crown

Even if you don't use tubular forms for the body of your footings, you can create smooth, symmetrical appearance on the exposed portion of the footing by setting a 3 to 4 in. high section of tubular form on top of the loosely poured footing, then fill the form section and striking it off with a screed board.

FIGURE H: Run a short screed board (like a section of 2 × 4) over the top of the form to knock off excess concrete and create a flat, smooth surface.

FIGURE I: Reattach layout lines to the batterboards and drop a plumb bob down to locate the center of each tube. Insert a J-bolt into the wet concrete, leaving 1 in. of the threaded end above the surface.

Ledgers

Ledger boards are secured to the rim joist of a house to support attached decks. For small, low-level decks (100 square feet or less), the ledger can be the same size as the joists (typically a 2 × 6); on large decks, elevated (second-story) decks, or decks that will support heavy loads or additional structures, use a 2 × 8 or 2 × 10 ledger. In all cases, check local building codes to make sure your ledger board is in compliance.

In conventional wood frame construction, lag screws are used to attach the ledger to the rim joist of the house (typically a 2 × 10 or 2 × 12) behind the exterior siding and sheathing—the second story also contains a rim joist that's level with the second-floor floor joists. Do not attach the ledger to siding, wall studs, or stud wall sole plates.

Depending on the structural details of the house and the desired deck height, the joists can either rest on top of the ledger or be hung flush with it, using joist hangers. For free-standing decks, use an additional beam and header joist and back corner posts to take the place of the ledger.

Locating the ledger

In all cases, use your drawings as a guide to cut the ledger to length. Note that ledger will be 3 in. shorter than the overall width of the deck framing, to allow for attachment of the two end joists to the ends of the ledger. Locate the ledger so the finished deck surface will be 1 in. below the interior floor level or door sill. This will prevent water from entering the house through the door opening. Measure down 1 in. from the sill, then add the thickness of the deck boards to indicate the top edge of the ledger. Mark with a pencil. On wood frame houses, this should also place the ledger directly opposite the floor header joist on the other side of the exterior siding. If you're not sure of the header joist location, transfer the height of the interior floor level to the outside wall by measuring down from a nearby window or doorway. From this point, measure down 6 in., which should roughly indicate the center point of the header.

With a helper, align the top edge of the ledger to your mark, then brace or tack the ledger against the house wall. If the house has wood siding, tack the ledger to the wall with one duplex nail at the center; use a 2-ft. level to level the ledger, then tack nails at both ends. For solid masonry walls, stucco walls or masonry veneer walls, build temporary braces from 2 × 4s to hold the ledger in place.

ATTACHING LEDGERS TO LAP SIDING WALLS

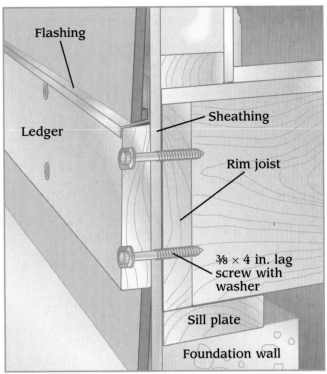

Attaching a ledger to an exterior wall with lap siding is a relatively uncomplicated task. See the projects description on pages 120 to 121.

ATTACHING LEDGERS TO STUCCO WALLS

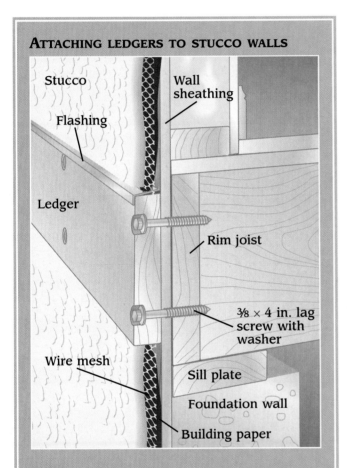

Cut the ledger to length, then brace it in position against the stucco wall, aligned with the rim joist of the house. Outline the ledger onto the stucco, then add 1½ in. at each end of the outline for the end joists. Remove the ledger. Install a masonry cutting blade in your circular saw and set it to about ¾ in. cutting depth (the average thickness of stucco skins). Cut along the outline, stopping the cut short of the corners. Finish the cuts with a cold chisel and maul. Remove the stucco material, then cut through the wire mesh stucco underlay with aviator snips. Clear all the debris from the cutout area until you've exposed the wall sheathing in front of the rim joist. Finish installing the ledger as you would with lap siding (See pages 119 to 121).

ATTACHING LEDGERS TO CONCRETE

Cut the ledger to length, then drill pairs of countersunk guide holes, spaced about 2 ft. apart, to accept ⅜ × 4 in. lag screws. Brace the ledger against the wall, level it, then outline it, adding 1½ in. on each side for the end joists. Drill through the guide holes with a small masonry bit 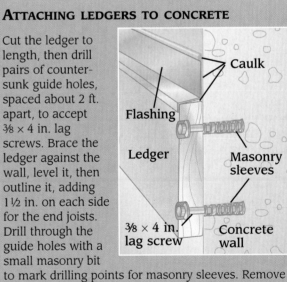 to mark drilling points for masonry sleeves. Remove the ledger. Drill ⅝ in. × 3 in. deep holes for masonry sleeves at the drilling points. Attach the ledger to the wall with lag screws driven through the guide holes and into the sleeves. Apply a heavy bead of polyurethane caulk between the top edge of the ledger and the wall, and another just above it. Cut flashing to fit (See page 120). Press the flashing firmly into the caulk bed. Run a bead of caulk across the top edge of the flashing. Cover the screw heads with caulk.

FIGURE A: Cut away the siding within the ledger layout area using a circular saw fitted with the proper blade. Set the blade depth to cut through the siding only.

FIGURE B: Cut the ledger board to size and mark each joist location on the ledger with a carpenter's square. Typical joist spacing is 16 in. on-center.

FIGURE C: Cut a strip of galvanized metal flashing to fit the length of the cutout area and slip the vertical flange up behind the flashing.

Attaching a ledger board

The following step-by-step photos show how to attach a ledger to a conventional wood frame house with wood, metal, vinyl or hardboard lap siding. Details for attaching ledgers to a masonry wall (such as a block foundation) or to stucco are discussed on page 119.

1 Mark a horizontal line ¼ in. above the top of the ledger outline you marked when laying out your deck footing locations (See pages 108 to 112). This additional space will leave room for installing a strip of galvanized flashing above the ledger. Remove the siding to accommodate the ledger board, flashing, end joist and fascia board, following your layout lines **(See FIGURE A).** NOTE: *For vinyl, wood or hardboard lapped siding, cut away the siding using a circular saw fitted with a carbide-toothed combination blade. If your siding is aluminum or steel, be sure to outfit the saw with a blade appropriate for cutting non-ferrous metals.* Regardless of the siding

TIP:
Flashing
alternative

If you find it difficult or impractical to install galvanized flashing behind your home's siding, here's an easy alternative. When you install the lag screws or bolts through the ledger board, insert 6 galvanized washers over the lag screw shaft so that once the ledger is installed, the washers are sandwiched between the ledger and the siding. The washers will provide a gap that allows water to run freely behind the ledger and air to circulate, keeping the back face of the ledger dry. Be sure to keep the gap free from leaves and other debris that could trap water and defeat the purpose.

composition, set the blade depth to match the thickness of the siding only, so that you do not damage the wall sheathing beneath.

2 Use a hammer and wood chisel to finish the cuts at each corner of the cutout area that the saw blade can't reach. Square up the corners. Then install a strip of building paper to cover the sheathing behind the siding and staple it into place.

3 Measure and cut the ledger to size from 2× dimensional treated lumber. The width of your ledger board will vary, depending on the size of the joists you'll be installing—the ledger width should match or exceed the joist width. Test-fit the ledger in the cutout area. Mark joist locations on the ledger, using a carpenter's square **(See FIGURE B).** Typical joist spacing is 16 in. on-center.

4 Cut preformed galvanized drip flashing to fit the length of the cutout and slide the top edge behind the siding **(See FIGURE C).** Don't use fasteners to hold the flashing in place in place.

5 Set the ledger into the cutout so that the flashing wraps over the top. Level the ledger and temporarily tack it in place with several 3-in. framing nails or duplex nails. Mark the ledger for pairs of ⅜ × 4-in. galvanized lag screws, spaced every 2 ft. along the length of the ledger. Drill a ⅜-in. pilot hole for each lag screw, through the ledger board and sheathing and into the rim joist of the house **(See FIGURE D).**

6 Slip a washer over each lag screw and install the the screws with a socket wrench to secure the ledger to the house **(See FIGURE E).**

7 Run a thick bead of heavy-duty silicone or polyurethane caulk along the joint between the flashing and the siding to seal out moisture **(See FIGURE F).** It's a good idea to caulk the cracks along the sides and bottom of the ledger as well.

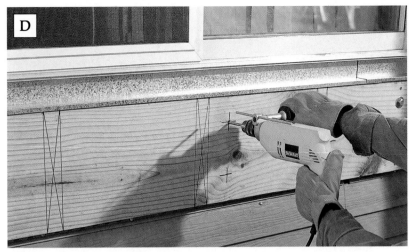

FIGURE D: Tack the ledger into place in the cutout area with framing nails or duplex nails. Mark the ledger for pairs of lag screws and drill a pilot hole for each screw.

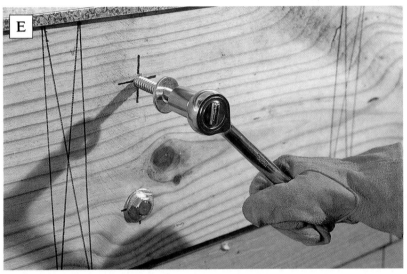

FIGURE E: Use a socket wrench to drive the lag screws that secure the ledger to the house. Use washers with the lag screws.

FIGURE F: Seal the joint between the flashing and the siding with a bead of heavy-duty silicone or polyurethane caulk.

Framing

Framing is the part of the deckbuilding process where your project actually begins to look like a deck. It's also labor-intensive and utterly critical to success. The framework of a deck, sometimes called the *undercarriage,* consists of a front joist called a header joist or rim joist, end or side joists, beams on some deck styles, and field joists that span between the header joist and the ledger, supporting the decking.

There's no single right way to frame a deck. Among the many variables are whether you're building a simple platform deck or a cantilevered deck; the size and height of the deck; the decking pattern you've selected; the number of levels in the deck project; whether the deck is free-standing or attached to a ledger on the house; and even whether or not you are bothered by the appearance of bulky galvanized deck hardware.

The order in which you install the frame members can also vary, depending on the project plan and the topographical features of the building site. The traditional method is to trim the post tops to level first, then attach beams or a header joist to the posts, parallel to the ledger. Then, the end joists and field joists are filled in between the beams or the header joist and the ledger. One drawback to this sequence is that it forces you to get the post heights exactly right, or the joists may not be square to the ledger and beams when you're finished. One way around this problem is to install the end joists first, supporting and leveling them in front with temporary braces. Once you know they're square and level, you can use them as a reference to mark cutting heights on the post tops, then finish the installation of the frame.

Using temporary braces to support the joists and even the header joists or beams is a particularly good idea when building on steep slopes or irregular terrain, where finding a reference point to measure from can be difficult. Weigh your framing options carefully before jumping in, from which type of fasteners to use to which assembly strategy you'd like to employ.

Anatomy of a deck frame

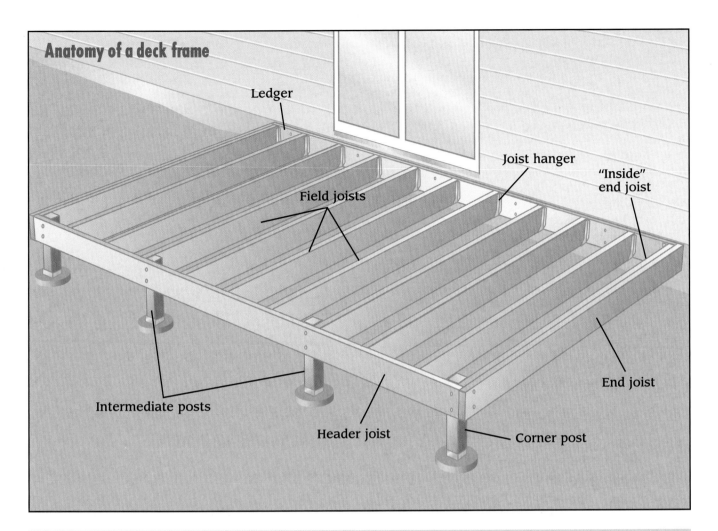

Ledger

Joist hanger

"Inside" end joist

Field joists

End joist

Intermediate posts

Header joist

Corner post

Cantilevered decks

A cantilevered deck is one that is supported by posts and a main beam that runs parallel to the ledger board. The beam is positioned back from the front edge of the deck, which extends past the beam as much as one-third of its total length. Cantilevered decks are popular choices when building on slopes or building a deck with a high elevation. This is mostly because the undercarriage of a cantilevered deck consumes less real estate than a deck built with corner posts in front. The positioning of the main beam is the most crucial step when building a cantilevered deck. The top of the beam must be level with the bottom of the ledger board (if the ledger is the same thickness as the joists). This means that the posts supporting the beam must be level.

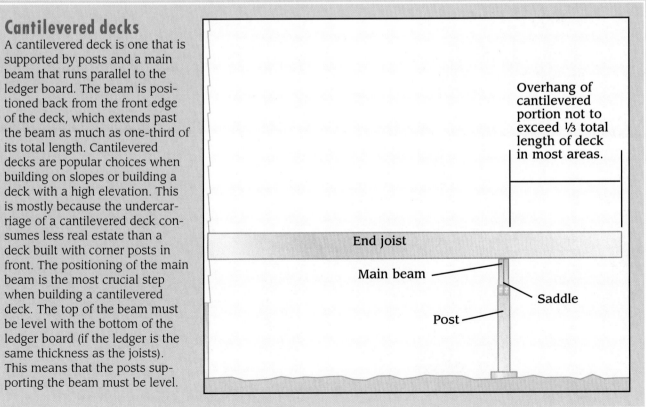

Overhang of cantilevered portion not to exceed ⅓ total length of deck in most areas.

End joist

Main beam

Saddle

Post

Options for joining frame members

There are nearly as many ways to fasten structural framing members as there are different styles of deck designs. Choosing the best method for your deck depends on the planned height of the deck (some methods will raise beams too high) and the type of fasteners used elsewhere on the deck—try to keep consistent. Whether you're installing a single or double beam also plays an important role in the decision. If you're using a double beam, try to select a fastening method where the beams are sandwiched together face-to-face, rather than attached to opposite sides of the post. In most cases, this means the doubled beam will rest atop the posts (the preferred arrangement). Where possible and practical, use metal fasteners. Make sure any end joints are supported from below.

SINGLE BEAM ATTACHED TO NARROW POST WITH LAG SCREWS

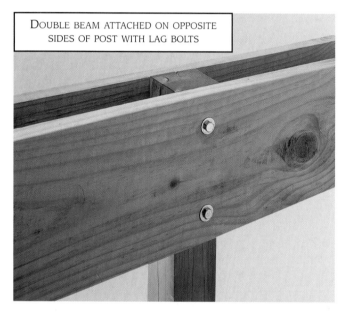

DOUBLE BEAM ATTACHED ON OPPOSITE SIDES OF POST WITH LAG BOLTS

SINGLE BEAM ATTACHED TO NARROW POST WITH T-STRAP

DOUBLE BEAM ATTACHED TO POST WITH BEAM SADDLE

SINGLE BEAM ATTACHED TO NARROW POST WITH SADDLE

SPLICED BEAM REINFORCED
WITH T-STRAPS

SPLICED BEAM REINFORCED
WITH PLYWOOD GUSSET

JOIST TOE-NAILED TO BEAM

JOIST HUNG WITH
JOIST HANGER

JOISTS WITH SPLICE
OVERLAPPING ON BEAM

JOISTS SPLICED WITH
JOIST STRAP

FIGURE A: Cover the project area that will be beneath the deck with landscape fabric. Weight the fabric down with dirt to hold it in place (if your deck is elevated more than 3 or 4 ft., ignore this step).

FIGURE B: Cut end joists to length, then align one end of a joist against the end of the ledger. Tack the end joist to the ledger with a 3-in. deck screw.

Framing a deck

The construction techniques for this particular deck are a departure from the "norm" in that the doubled end and rim joists take the place of beams, with single joists of the same dimension hung between them. These perimeter members were installed and braced prior to cutting and setting the posts, so that we could cut and locate the posts with greater accuracy. The top end of each 6 × 6 post is notched to provide additional support for the beams.

The main platform consists of 2 × 12 beams and joists, attached to a 2 × 12 ledger. The lower platform consists of 2 × 10 beams and joists attached to the upper platform. For a lighter-duty deck, you can get away with 2 × 8 joists.

The following steps show how to construct the main platform only, although you'll notice that a second ledger is in place for the lower platform. Use the same procedures to build the lower platform. The beefed-up main platform was designed to carry the weight of an enclosed three-season porch, which will be added at a future date.

1 Roll sheets of landscape fabric over the deck project area to to inhibit weed growth beneath the deck **(See FIGURE A).** Cut the fabric around cement footings to keep the tops exposed and weight the fabric down along the seams and edges with dirt. In areas where termites are a problem, treat the project area with insecticide first.

2 Cut the end joists to length, according to your deck plan drawings. Construct temporary 2 × 4 braces attached to a plywood "foot" to support the joist near the end opposite the ledger. With your helper holding up one end of the joist, attach the other end flush to the end of the ledger near the top edge with a 3-in. deck screw **(See FIGURE B).**

3 Set a carpenter's level on top of the joist at the far end and level the joist by pivoting it up or down. Once it's level, fasten it to the 2 × 4 brace with several 3-in. deck screws **(See FIGURE C).** Repeat this process on the other end of the ledger to position a second end joist that is parallel to the first.

4 Screw the header joist flush to the ends of the end joists with 3-in. deck screws, spaced about 2 in. apart along the width of the header joist **(See FIGURE D).** Have a helper hold the opposite end of the joist while you drive the screws. *NOTE: You may need to shift the end joists one way or the other in order to align them with the header joist.* Once the header joist is secured to the end joists, drive additional deck screws through the end joists at the ledger every 2 in.

FIGURE C: Level the end joist near the far end with a carpenter's level and fasten the leveled joist to a temporary 2 x 4 support brace with several deck screws. Hang and level the other end joist to the ledger now.

FIGURE D: Cut the header joist to length, align it with the ends of the two end joists and fasten it in place with 3-in. galvanized deck screws, spaced at 2 in. intervals.

FIGURE E: Fasten diagonal supports to the 2 × 4 braces with a deck screw. Each diagonal support is outfitted with a stake at the opposite end, which is driven into the ground.

Overlap the "inside" joists at the corner post locations

FIGURE F: Reinforce the end and header joists by attaching a second joist to each on the inside face. Fasten the members together with deck screws in a staggered pattern. Overlap the ends of the "inside" joists at the corner post locations.

Pneumatic nail guns, powered by compressed air, are a suitable (and faster) alternative to deck building with screws. For heavy framing applications through 2× lumber, use 2¾-in. galvanized nails. Wear eye protection when using pneumatic nailers and follow all safety precautions.

5 Steady the deck assembly by screwing a diagonal brace to each 2 × 4 brace holding up the end joists. Attach a 12-in. stake to the opposite end of the diagonal brace with a deck screw and drive the stake into the ground. Then attach the diagonal brace to the vertical 2 × 4 brace with a deck screw **(See FIGURE E).**

6 For larger decks like this project deck, reinforce the perimeter joists by doubling them up. Attach a second joist inside the header and end joists with 3-in. deck screws, spaced every 2 ft. in a staggered pattern and screwed from inside the deck frame outward **(See FIGURE F).** (You can also laminate joists together and frame the deck with nails. See *TIP,* left). Overlap these "inside" joists in the corners where the header joist meets the end joists. Attach the "inside" joists to the ledger by driving 3-in. deck screws toe-nail style (diagonally) into the ledger.

7 Attach a mason's line along the length of the header joist, and set it off from the outside face of the joist with a spacer (such as a deck screw) at each end **(See FIGURE G).** Pull the string line taut and tie it off to a screw on either end of the header joist. Since most dimension lumber has a natural bow to it, the line will be used in the next step as a reference to straighten the double header joist.

FIGURE G: Attach a mason's line along the length of the header joist, and set it off from the outside face of the joist with a spacer. We used deck screws for spacers.

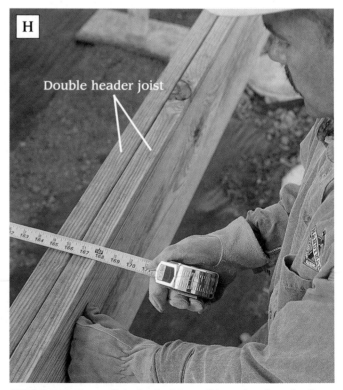

FIGURE H: Push or pull the header joist until it touches the string line, straightening the header joist. Measure the distance between the ledger and the inside face of the header to determine the length of the first "field" joist.

8 Push or pull the header joist near the middle of its span until it touches the reference line. Hold it in place. Measure the distance between the ledger (at the nearest joist or beam site marked on the ledger) and the inside face of the header joist and note this distance **(See FIGURE H).** Use this measurement to cut the first "field" joist or double beam to length.

9 Mark the location for the middle joist or beam (determined in *Step 8*) on the inside face of the header joist **(See FIGURE I).** Align and attach one side of a joist hanger to the header joist and ledger at the middle joist or beam layout marks, using 1¼-in. galvanized joist-hanger nails.

10 Set the center joist or beam into the joist hangers. Press the "loose" side of each hanger snug against the joist or beam to cradle it, align the hanger with the layout marks, then attach the hanger to the ledger and header joist with 1¼ in. joist-hanger nails. Fasten the hanger to the joist or beam with more nails **(See FIGURE J).** Drive a nail into each hole on the hangers. Check the entire deck frame for square by measuring the diagonals, and adjust the deck frame as needed by shifting the temporary braces and stakes until the diagonal measurements are equal. The deck platform is now square.

FIGURE I: Align and attach one side of a joist hanger to the header joist and ledger at the middle joist or beam layout marks, using 1¼-in. galvanized joist-hanger nails .

FIGURE J: Set the joist or beam into the hanger, align the loose side of the hanger with the joist layout mark, and fasten the hanger to the header, and then to the joist or beam, with 1¼-in. joist-hanger nails.

FIGURE K: Secure a metal post hanger to the J-bolt embedded in each concrete footing with a nut and washer. Tighten the nuts with a socket wrench.

FIGURE L: Measure up from each post anchor to determine the *overall height* and *notch height* for each post.

FIGURE M: Trim each post to length by first cutting along all four faces at the post-end cutting line, using a circular saw set to maximum depth. If the thickness of your posts is less than that of our project deck posts, you may be able to complete these cuts with a circular saw alone.

Installing posts

11 Attach a galvanized post anchor to each concrete deck footing, securing it to the embedded J-bolt with a nut and washer **(See FIGURE K).**

12 Measure up from the bottom of each footing post anchor to the top edge of the deck frame in order to determine the overall height for each post. Take a second measurement from the bottom of the post anchor to the bottom edge of the deck frame. This measurement indicates where each post will be notched so the deck joists can rest on the posts **(See FIGURE L).**

13 Mark the post lengths and the notch locations on the faces of each post so you can cut all the posts at one time. *Note: For our project deck, we used 6 × 6 treated posts and cut notches in two faces for corner posts and one face for intermediate posts.* For large posts like these, set your circular saw to its maximum blade depth and cut along all four faces of each post to begin to trim them to length **(See FIGURE M).**

14 Because most circular saws cannot cut through a 6 × 6, even when cutting through all four faces, complete the cuts made in *Step 13* with a reciprocating saw or hand saw to cut the posts to length **(See FIGURE N).**

15 Start the notch cuts in each post with your circular saw set to maximum depth **(See FIGURE O),** then finish the notch cuts where the circular saw can't reach with a reciprocating saw or hand saw **(See FIGURE P).** Clean up the inside corners of each notch with a hand saw or wood chisel and hammer so the joists will rest cleanly on the posts. *Note: Photos O through R illustrate the procedure for notching and attaching a corner post.*

16 At each post location, fit the posts under the joists and into the post anchors on the concrete footings. Clamp a level to each post and adjust it to plumb, then nail the post to the post anchor with 6d galvanized common nails. Drill pilot holes through the posts and into the deck frame joists to accept two ⅜ × 4-in. lag screws with washers **(See FIGURE Q).** Fit each lag screw with a washer and drive the lag screws through the posts and into the joists to fasten them together **(See FIGURE R).** Once all the posts are attached to the deck, remove the 2 × 4 braces from the end joists.

17 Mark the remaining "field" joist locations along the inside of the header joist to match those you've marked on the ledger. Install a joist hanger on the ledger and header joist at each marked field joist

FIGURE N: Complete the cuts started in FIGURE M with a reciprocating saw or hand saw, if necessary, to finish trimming the posts to length.

FIGURE O: Start the notch cuts in each post by following the notch cutting lines with your circular saw set to maximum depth. In this photo, we're cutting the notches for a corner post.

FIGURE P: Finish the notch cuts where the circular saw can't reach with a reciprocating saw or hand saw. Clean up the notched areas with a wood chisel or hand saw so that the joists will sit squarely and evenly in the notches.

FIGURE Q: Set each post into place so the joists are resting in the post notches and the post bottoms are sitting in the post anchors. Plumb the posts with a level, nail them to the post anchors and drill ⅜-in. pilot holes through the posts and into the joists for lag screws.

FIGURE R: Fasten the posts to the joists with 4-in. lag screws fitted with washers. Install two lag screws per post, using a socket wrench.

FIGURE S: Attach galvanized joist hangers along the ledger and the header joists for hanging the field joists. Cut the joists to length, set them on the joist hangers and fasten them in place with joist-hanger nails.

FIGURE T: Prepare joists for angled installations by setting them into position over adjoining joists and marking the angles where the joists intersect on either end.

FIGURE U: Set your circular saw to match the angles you marked on the joist and make the end cuts.

location, then follow the procedure outlined in *Steps 9 and 10* to secure the field joists to the deck frame **(See FIGURE S).**

18 Some deck designs may incorporate angled corners into deck platforms to add visual appeal. We used angled header joists in the lower platform of our project deck. Prepare joists for angled installations by setting them into position over adjoining joists and marking the angles where the joists intersect on either end **(See FIGURE T).** Then set the angle on your circular saw to match the angle marks on the joist ends and make the end cuts **(See FIGURE U).** Joist hangers are available to match several regular angles used in deck construction. Attach the angled hangers to adjoining joists first with 1¼-in. galvanized joist nails, then set the angled joists into position on the joist hangers and fasten them in place **(See FIGURE V).**

FIGURE V: Attach angled joist hangers to adjoining joists with 1¼-in. galvanized joist-hanger nails. Then set the angled joist (or joists) into the hangers and fasten them in place.

The completed deck frame may be a little unconventional, but it's exceptionally sturdy and ready to take on the load of the three-season porch that is planned for the upper deck (someday).

Decking

Laying decking is probably the most satisfying part of the deckbuilding process. It goes quickly and provides a sense that the project is nearly complete. However, because the decking is the part that "shows," you'll want to take extra care when you install the boards. The deck will have a nicer, neater appearance if you strike a chalk line across the boards at nail or screw locations and use the lines as a guide to keep the fasteners in neat rows.

If you want to apply a wood preservative or another protective finish to the substructure or to the undersides of the deck boards, apply it before attaching the decking. Also, if you're incorporating benches or railings into the deck, attach the uprights or posts before laying the decking (See pages 146 to 157).

If possible, buy deck boards that are long enough to span the entire width of the deck. If you do need to butt boards in each run, stagger the joints, making sure they fall directly over a joist. Leave a ½-in. space between board ends to allow for wood expansion and contraction.

Deck boards can be laid in many interesting patterns (See pages 104 to 105). Note that most patterns other than simple straight rows require special joist layouts for support. You can use 2 × 6 lumber or 2 × 4 lumber (cedar, redwood, cypress and pressure-treated are the most common), or you can use 1¼ in. thick premilled deck boards (See page 102).

The subject of which deck board face should face up is currently under evaluation. Traditionally, deckbuilders have always installed boards with the bark side facing up, presuming that if the boards cup from exposure to moisture the cupping will be directed against the joist, preventing the surface of the deck from becoming uneven. But some industry experts assert that modern kiln-drying methods alter the character of the wood enough to reverse the direction of the cupping, so the boards actually cup toward the bark side. While everyone seems to have an opinion on the subject, the fact is that most professional deck builders pay little attention to which board face is facing upward.

Installing the decking

1 Start laying deck boards at the ledger side of the deck. Choose the straightest deck boards for the first row of decking and cut them to length so their ends overhang the outside edges of the end joists slightly—the best way to get a straight line at the sides of the deck is to trim the boards, using a straightedge guide, after they're all in place. Space the first row of decking about ⅛ in. away from the house siding. Screw the first row of decking to the joists and ledger with 2½-in. galvanized deck screws. Fasten additional rows of decking with pairs of deck screws at each joist location, centering the screws on the joists and setting the screws about 1 in. in from the edges of each deck board. Use 16d common nails as spacers between the rows **(See FIGURE A).**

2 Arrange deck boards so that all splices (end joints) fall directly over a joist, and splices are not aligned on consecutive boards. Butt the board ends together so the seam falls midway across the joist. When driving screws close to board ends, drill pilot holes first **(See FIGURE B).**

3 Warped deck boards can be forced into alignment with the straight boards. Position the warped board so the concave edge faces away from the fastened

Drill driver tip options

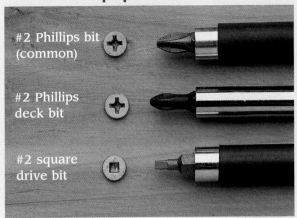

#2 Phillips bit (common)

#2 Phillips deck bit

#2 square drive bit

Three primary drill/driver bit styles are available for driving deck screws. A common #2 Phillips bit will easily drive deck screws through cedar or redwood decking without a pilot hole, but you may want to drill pilots if installing treated lumber. Specialty deck bits feature a hardened tip to withstand the torque that develops when you drive a screw through treated decking or 2× framing members. Square-drive screws are considerably more expensive than Phillips head screws, but they're less prone to stripping.

How to lay decking

FIGURE A: Fasten rows of decking, starting from the ledger side of the deck. Use 2½-in. galvanized deck screws, with 16d nails inserted as spacers between the rows.

FIGURE B: Center board splices directly over a joist, with the seam between the boards located midway across the joist. Drill pilot holes for the screws to keep the board ends from splitting.

FIGURE C: Use a 2 × 4 lever to straighten warped boards. Tack the 2 × 4 to the joist, using a single screw. Pivot the board forward against the warped board to force it into alignment with the rest of the boards.

rows of decking. Fasten a piece of 2 × 4 to the end joist, butted up against the warped board by driving a single screw through the 2 × 4 into the inside face of the joist. Insert nail spacers between the warped board and the fastened row, then force the end of the warped board toward the fastened board by pressing the 2 × 4 against it, using the screw as a pivot **(See FIGURE C)**. Drive deck screws to secure the board before it springs back. If the warp is severe, you may need to straighten the board at additional joist locations.

4 Proceed to lay rows of decking until you are within eight to ten rows from the end. Measure out to the end of the deck from the last row installed. Calculate the number of rows, including spaces, that it will take to reach the front of the deck, then mark the positions of each row on the joists **(See FIGURE D)**. Adjust the spacing, if needed, so the outside edge of the last deck board row will end up flush with the end of the deck.

5 Snap a chalk line along the ends of the overhanging deck boards, about 1/16 in. beyond the outside edge of the end joists. Use a circular saw to trim off the overhanging boards, following the chalk line **(See FIGURE E)**. Set the blade depth so the saw barely cuts through the decking to avoid marring the face of the end joists with the blade.

FIGURE D: About eight rows before the edge of the deck, measure the distance from the last row of installed boards to the edge. Calculate how many boards you'll need (include 1/8 in. for gaps between boards). Adjust the spacing if possible to avoid rip-cutting any deck boards.

FIGURE E: Snap a chalk line across the ends of the installed boards to mark a trimming line on each end of the deck. Trim the boards with a circular saw (use a straightedge for maximum accuracy). Take care to avoid cutting into the joist below the ends of the decking.

Installing decking around posts

STEP 1: Lay rows of decking until you are within one deck board's width from the post. Measure the distance from the edge of the closest fastened deck board to the face of the post.

STEP 2: Press a deck board up against the post. Draw a cutting line on the board face, parallel to the edge. The distance from the line to the edge of the board should be the same distance measured in STEP 1. Extend the lines created by the faces of the post onto the deck board until they meet the cutting line.

STEP 3: To cut out the notch, drill holes at the inside corners of the outline, then cut along the outline with a jig saw, connecting the holes. Square up the corners of the notch with a chisel or file.

STEP 4: Set the deck board into place and adjust the cutout area, if needed, until the board fits snugly around the post. Fasten it into place with deck screws.

Stairs

Decks higher than about 8 in. above grade will need at least one step to provide access between the deck and ground level. Steps also serve as a connection between two deck levels. If only one or two steps are needed, you can build a set of box steps which, as the name implies, are simple wooden boxes with deck boards on the top to create stair treads.

If three or more steps are required, you'll need to build a more conventional stairway in which the steps are attached to a set of stringers. The stringers are typically cut from 2 × 12s, which are secured to the deck joists or beams at the top end, and anchored to a footing at ground level. On outdoor stairs, the treads are made from 2 × 4s, 2 × 6s, or 2 × 8s attached to the stringers—wider boards, such as 2 × 10s or 2 × 12s tend to cup or warp when employed as single stair treads, thus are not recommended for exterior steps. Some stairways also incorporate risers to enclose the space between the treads as you typically see on interior stairs.

Building stairs, especially in longer runs, can get tricky. There are plenty of mathematic formulas to help you develop your design, but in the end it usually comes down to trial-and-error.

Basic design guidelines

Generally, outdoor stairs are not as steep as indoor stairs, having proportionally wider treads and lower rises. The staircase itself is also wider. For general access, the clear width between outer stingers should be at least 36 in. A stairway 5 ft. wide will accommodate two people side by side. All stairways wider than 4 ft. should include a third stringer placed midway between the two outside stringers, but installing a third stringer is also a good idea for prolonging the life of narrower staircase.

To build a comfortable set of stairs, you'll need to establish a suitable rise-to-run ratio: *Rise* refers to the height between the steps; *run* refers to the depth of the step, minus any overhang. As a general rule for outdoor stairs, the tread width (run) in inches plus twice the step height (rise) in inches should equal 24 to 26 inches. For exterior stairs, the rise (vertical distance between treads) should be between 4½ in. and 7 in. The tread depth should be a minimum of 11 in. Building codes often dictate acceptable run/rise relationships. In most deck situations, treads consist of two 2 × 6s, spaced ¼ in. apart, to create a tread run of 11¼ in. In this case, the formulas tell us that the riser height should be between 6½ and 7 in. This is the most common and useful outdoor step relationship.

The real trick to designing stairs comes when you try to actually incorporate the run and rise ratios into your design. By code, all stairs in a flight must have the same rise and run proportions (this is a safety issue: non-uniform sizing of stairs confuse our feet in a hurry and can easily cause injury from falls).

Measuring for stairs

To calculate the actual run and rise and the number of steps needed, first measure the vertical distance between the deck surface and the ground or between deck levels (total rise). Divide the total rise by the rough riser height (7 in. is a good starting point): the result is about the number of stairs you'll need in the staircase. More often than not, however, this formula usually results in a number of steps that is not a whole number. If this is the case, divide the whole number of steps into the total rise to get the exact riser height. Note that the number of stair treads required is always one less than the number of risers—the top "step" is the deck surface.

Next, multiply the exact riser height by two and subtract it from the overall ratio figure of 24 to 26 in. This will yield the ideal tread depth in the 10 to 12 in. range.

Finally, calculate the total run or *span* by multiplying the tread depth by the number of risers minus one. Knowing the span will enable you to identify and mark the bottom end of the staircase. If the stairs don't fit the space, adjust the tread/riser ratio by increasing one while decreasing the other. If this results in a tread/riser ratio that does not conform to acceptable limits you may need to redesign the stairway. For instance, on tall decks or steep hillside decks, you can use an "L" or "U"-shaped flight of stairs running parallel to the deck and incorporating one or more landings, rather than having a straight run of stairs running perpendicular to the deck.

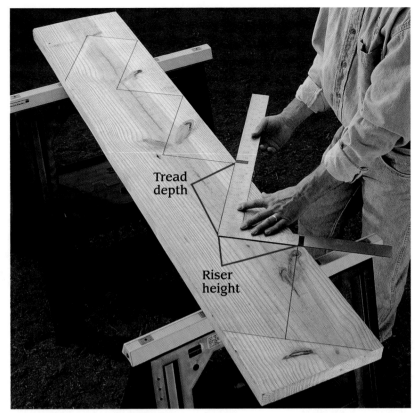

Note the riser and tread dimensions on a framing square and use the square as a layout tool for marking cutting lines or layout lines on the stair stringers.

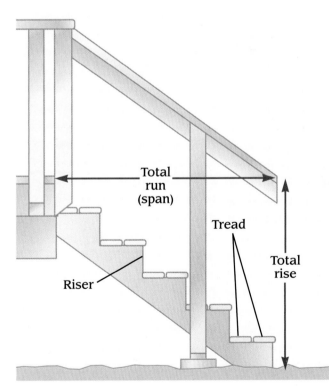

Designing stairs involves a little math and a little trial-and-error. The trick is to come up with a plan that has uniformly sized risers and treads that are in formation and terminate at a convenient location on the low end of the flight.

FIGURE A: Measure the overall height between deck platforms to determine the rise and run of the stairs. Be sure to take into account the thickness of the decking if you haven't already installed it.

FIGURE B: Use both legs of a framing square (one leg for rise and the other leg for run) to lay out a template stair stringer on a length of treated 2 × 12, according to your rise/run calculations. Mark waste areas with an "X".

Building deck stairs

Our project deck uses a system of "wraparound" stairs that provide easy access from all sides of both deck platforms. Every deck project will, of course, require its own unique stair system, depending upon the number of levels there are to the deck, its elevation from the ground and the deck's basic style. The following pages serve as an example for how to build wraparound-style steps for a low-standing, two-tiered deck. Modify your stair plans as necessary to accommodate the specific needs of your deck project.

1 Measure the overall rise between the two deck levels and use this distance to determine the rise/run ratio, following the formula discussed on page 139 **(See FIGURE A).** *NOTE: Be sure to allow for the thickness of the decking you plan to use if the decking on either deck platform isn't installed.*

2 Use both legs of a framing square (one leg for rise and the other leg for run) to lay out a template stair stringer on a length of treated 2 × 12, following your rise/run calculations **(See FIGURE B).** Be sure to account for the thickness of your treads and risers when laying out the stringer. Mark the waste side of the cuts with an "X" to keep your layout orientation clear. *TIP: For longer stringer layouts than shown here, mark the legs of your carpenter's square with pieces of tape to serve as quick layout references.*

3 Cut out the stringer with a hand saw, reciprocating saw or circular saw. If you use a circular saw, finish the inside corners with a hand saw where the circular blade won't reach **(See FIGURE C).** Set the template stringer into place on the deck and check it for accuracy. Then use it to mark the remaining stringers and cut them all to shape. Plan to install a stringer every 16 in. along the width of the stairway.

4 Set a stringer into place and level it. If the edge of the stringer that butts against the joist extends below the joist, measure down from the top of the joist to the top diagonal edge of the stringer **(See FIGURE D).** Use this measurement to determine the width of a plywood nailer that will support the top ends of the stringers where they rest against the perimeter joists.

5 Cut the nailers to size from ¾-in.-thick exterior treated plywood and attach them to the joist faces with rows of 2½-in. galvanized deck screws, spaced 10 to 12 in. apart, along the length of the joists **(See FIGURE E).** Use a tape measure and try square to mark each stringer location on the plywood nailers.

6 Place the two outermost stringers of the stairway against the nailer, level and square them to the

FIGURE C: Cut a stringer to shape following the layout lines. This first stringer will serve as a template for marking and cutting out the other stringers.

FIGURE D: Set the top of the stringer against the end joist of the upper deck platform so that it rests on the lower deck. Measure down from the upper deck to the bottom of the stringer to determine the width of the plywood nailer.

Plywood nailer

FIGURE E: Cut the nailer to size from treated plywood and attach it to the face of the header or end joist with 2½-in. galvanized deck screws, spaced 10 to 12 in. apart along the length of the joist.

FIGURE F: Level and square the outermost stringers for a staircase, aligning them with the layout locations on the nailer. Mark the bottom front edge of each stringer where it meets the decking. Then snap a chalk line to serve as a reference for installing the toe-kick.

FIGURE G: Mark and notch all the lower front edges of the stringers to make way for the toe-kick. Cut the toe-kick board to length, align it with the chalk line and attach it to the decking with screws.

FIGURE H: Fasten the bottom ends of the stringers to the toe-kick with two 2½-in. galvanized screws driven diagonally into the toe-kick from each side.

nailer, and mark the bottom edges of both stringers where they meet the lower deck **(See FIGURE F).** Snap a chalk line between these marks. The chalk line represents the front edge of a 2 × 4 toe-kick board that will be notched into the front lower edge of each stringer to anchor the stringers to the lower deck. Since the stairway wraps around the deck, follow the same procedure using stringers and chalk lines to establish toe-kick reference lines on adjacent sides of the deck.

7 Measure 1½ by 3½-in. notches in the front bottom corner of each stringer for the toe-kick board and cut the notches out with a saw. Measure and cut the toe-kicks to length from treated lumber.

8 Mark stringer locations on the toe-kicks using the nailer as a reference. Align the toe-kicks with the chalk lines, and set a stringer in place to check your layout. Fasten the toe-kicks to the decking with 3-in. deck screws, spaced 1 ft. apart **(See FIGURE G).** NOTE: *Since the stairs wrap around the deck, the toe-kicks in our project deck butt against one another at the outside corners of the deck where the adjacent stairways meet.*

9 Align the stringers with the nailer and toe-kick lay-out marks and attach the top end of each stringer to the nailer with pairs of 2½-in. deck screws driven diagonally into the nailer. Another alternative is to use galvanized stringer brackets (See *OPTION*, below).

OPTION: Stringer brackets

Stringer brackets, which work like joist hangers, cradle the bottom of the stringer and provide nailing flanges for attaching the stringers to the deck joists. Use 1¼-in. joist-hanger nails for fasteners.

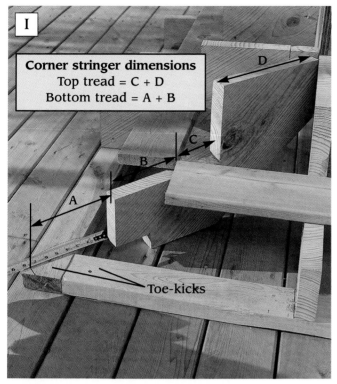

Corner stringer dimensions
Top tread = C + D
Bottom tread = A + B

D

C

B

A

Toe-kicks

FIGURE I: Set an extra stringer into position in an outside corner, align deck boards to the lower tread, and use the formulas outlined above to determine the dimensions for the corner stringer.

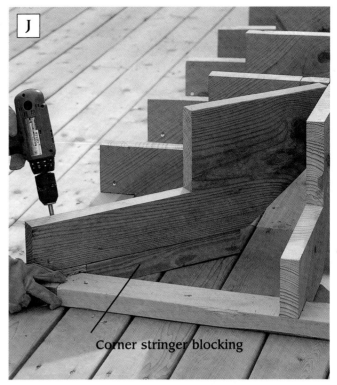

Corner stringer blocking

FIGURE J: Attach a length of extra blocking beneath corner stringers that are deeper than can be fabricated within the width of a 2 × 12. Fasten the corner stringers to the decking with screws.

10 Fasten the bottom end of the stringers to the toe-kick with two 2½-in. galvanized screws driven diagonally into the toe-kick from each side **(See FIGURE H).** Check each stringer with a carpenter's square before driving the screws to ensure that each stringer is perpendicular to the toe-kick.

11 Lay out and cut the corner stringer where adjacent stairways will meet. Establish the dimensions as follows: Set a spare stringer against the deck corner between the end stringers on the two adjacent staircases and line it up with the inside corner where the toe-kicks intersect. Lay two deck boards on the lower treads of adjacent stringers, tight against the riser edge of the stringer, and slide them until they intersect over the lower tread of the angled stringer **(See FIGURE I).** Then use the formulas in FIGURE I as references for determining tread depths. Distance A (starting 1 in. in from the outside toe-kick corner) plus distance B (front edge of the bottom tread to the corner where the deck boards intersect) equals the lower tread depth for the corner brace. Distance C (deck board intersection to stringer riser) plus distance D (top stringer tread) equals the top tread for the corner stringer. Add distances A through D to determine the overall length of the corner stringer. The riser heights remain the same.

FIGURE K: Construct treated-wood boxes for stairs that wrap around the end stringer of a stairway. Screw them to the stringer and to the decking with 2½-in. galvanized deck screws

FIGURE L: Measure and cut riser boards to fit each step leading up to the deck platform. Miter-cut riser-board ends at outside corners. Attach them to the stringers with 2½-in. galvanized deck screws.

FIGURE M: Cut and install the stair treads with pairs of 2½-in. deck screws, mitering the ends of the treads where they meet the corner stringers.

FIGURE N: Set 5 × 6 treated posts into 3-in.-deep trenches to serve as footings beneath box-frame steps. Be sure the tops of the posts are level in the trenches.

12 Cut the corner stringer to the proportions outlined in *Step 11*. The corner stringers for our project deck were so deep that they exceeded the width of a 2 × 12. We accounted for the extra width by fastening treated blocking beneath, extending the full width of the corner stringer base, less the corner width of the intersecting toe-kicks. Attach the corner stringers with 2½-in. deck screws driven toenail style into the deck **(See FIGURE J).**

13 Where stairs stop short of a deck corner or house wall, construct a treated wood box the same height as the bottom stringer tread, so that you can wrap the first step around the side of the end stringer and back to the end or header joist. Attach the box to the end stringer, upper deck, and lower deck with 2½-in. galvanized deck screws **(See FIGURE K).**

14 Measure and cut 1× or 2× riser boards (depending on your deck plan) to fit each step leading to the deck platform. Miter-cut the ends of the risers that meet at the corner stringers for a more finished appearance. Attach the risers to the stringers with 2½-in. deck screws, two screws per joint **(See FIGURE L).** If you plan to attach fascia boards to the deck, install them now in the same manner as the riser boards (See *OPTION*, next page).

15 Cut and install the stair treads with pairs of 2½-in. deck screws, mitering the ends of the

FIGURE O: Construct box frames that match the tread depth of the rest of the deck stairs. Set them on timber posts and screw the boxes to the deck joists.

FIGURE P: Attach stair treads to the tops of the box frames.

treads where they meet the corner stringers **(See FIG-URE M).** Use two tread boards of equal width for wide treads and butt the inside tread board against the riser. As with decking, splices between tread boards should occur directly over a framing member to provide adequate support. Drill pilot holes before driving screws near the ends of tread boards.

16 For our project deck, we chose box-frame steps to transition from the lower deck platform to the ground. Box-frame steps are not supported by concrete footings but normally rest directly on the ground. We decided to use 5 × 6 treated posts as "footings" beneath our box-frame steps and dug 3-in. trenches to set the posts half their thickness below grade **(See FIGURE N).** Be sure the posts are level in the trenches.

17 Construct treated-wood boxes that match the tread depth of the rest of the deck stairs. Miter-cut the ends of boxes that join at the deck corners. Snap chalk lines where the top edges of the boxes will meet the deck joists. Set the boxes onto the timber footings, align them to the chalk lines and attach the boxes to the deck joists with 2½-in. deck screws driven every 12 in. Reinforce the box frames with perpendicular "webs" spaced every 16 in. **(See FIGURE O).**

18 Attach tread boards to the tops of the box frames with 2½-in. deck screws, screwing into the webs. Use two screws per joint **(See FIGURE P).**

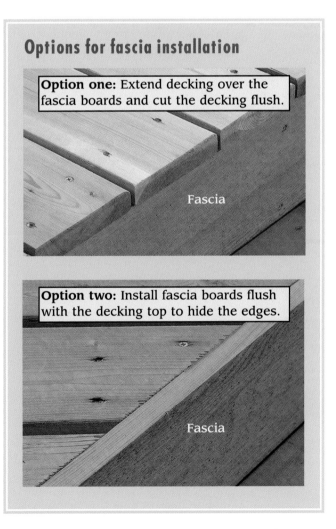

Options for fascia installation

Option one: Extend decking over the fascia boards and cut the decking flush.

Fascia

Option two: Install fascia boards flush with the decking top to hide the edges.

Fascia

Railings & accessories

The numerous photos of successful deck projects sprinkled throughout this book have a common characteristic that sets them apart from ordinary decks that have gone unnoticed: the accessories. Uniquely designed railings that echo the setting of the deck, built-in benches and planters, overhead arbor-and-trellis structures . . . it's in these original touches that a deck can truly stand out from the crowd.

While some deck accessories are mainly decorative or fulfill a nonessential function, railings are indispensable features that are required by building codes on any deck that's more than 30 in. above the grade. To protect deck occupants from falling and becoming injured, the deck railing should be at least 36 in. high. And recently, a lot of news has been made in the building trades about the revised rules governing the spacing of the balusters. Previously, balusters could be as far apart as 6 in. But it was determined that gaps of that width pose a safety risk to small children, who in many cases managed to get their heads wedged in between the balusters. Under current code, railing balusters must be no more than 4 in. apart (See page 149).

But in addition to safety protection, railings contribute much to the overall appearance of a deck by giving it strong vertical lines and sometimes new textures. The classic railing design features 2 × 2 balusters attached to stringers that run between posts. The upper stringer is usually treated with a cap rail. But more ambitious designers have found that there are many creative ways to shake up the classic look and add even more interest to your deck project. Step-downs and curves are two popular ways to create a custom appearance, as are selecting unique building materials and incorporating other features (such as planters or benches) into the railing structure.

When choosing a railing style and any other permanent deck accessories, try to develop designs that share some common features with other parts of your deck, house or yard.

A simple planter box presents a perfect opportunity to make good use of any leftover deck supplies.

Built-in benches can be supported by posts attached to the undercarriage of the deck, or suspended from heavy vertical members, as in the above deck that's attached to timbers supporting an arbor.

Railings amplify angles. If you've gone to the effort of creating a deck with a complex footprint, show off your carpentry abilities by adding a railing that commands attention, like the one shown to the left.

Accessories abound in this well-equipped deck. Built-in seating, an overhead arbor, finely crafted railings and even an outdoor kitchen center make for a very unique and efficient outdoor living space.

Non-traditional materials, like the galvanized tubing used to make horizontal siding on this deck, add new textures and a sense of fun.

Steep slopes require that you take extra care to create a sturdy railing structure that does not interfere with the view.

Post caps and finials add flair to railing posts and to newel posts (the end posts on step railings). Wood caps and finials should be of the same material as the rest of the railing, but contrasting metal caps can be used effectively.

Balusters can be made from plain 2 × 2 stock, or you can dress up railings by using premilled balusters with decorative profiles.

Molded handrails may be required to provide a convenient hand grasp for people using the stairs. Most fit over 2 × 2 railing stringers

Railing requirements

Most building codes require decks that are more than 30 in. above the ground to have railings. Stairways with three or more steps also must have railings on one, or sometimes both sides of the stairs. Many codes require that stair railings have a grippable handrail (See photo above). Typically railings must extend a minimum of 34 in. to 36 in. above the deck surface. They need to be strong enough to provide support when people lean against them or even sit on them. Also, the railing should not have openings wider than 4 in., to prevent toddlers from squeezing through the railing. The code restricting baluster spacing contains a simple test for enforcing the code: a 4-in.-dia. sphere must not be able to pass between any two balusters in the railing. Nor should it be able to pass between the lower stringer and the deck surface. To be on the safe side, lay out balusters so they're no more than about 3¾ in. apart.

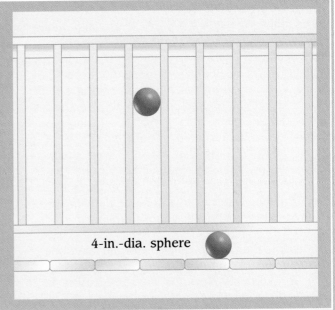

4-in.-dia. sphere

FIGURE A: Drill two 1-in.-dia., ½-in.-deep countersunk holes in the outside face of the notched area of each post, then drill a ⅜-in.-dia. pilot hole through each counterbore.

FIGURE B: Attach the top and bottom notched posts to the deck and the stair stringers with lag bolts. Check the posts with a carpenter's level to ensure that they're plumb.

Railings

The following pages show how to attach a railing to a short flight of steps. On stairways up to 8 ft. long, you'll need four posts—two at the top of the stairs (typically notched over the face of the end or header joist) and two at the bottom, fastened to the stringers near the first or second riser or anchored into the ground next to the stringers. On longer flights of stairs, you'll probably need to install a third post midway between the end posts. You can also adapt the stair railing design we show here to wrap railings around the perimeter of your deck, as we did for our project deck. Check building codes in your area for all railing requirements when you design your railings.

1 Measure the two railing posts for the top of the stairway and cut the posts to length—we used 4 × 4s for our posts. ***Note: be sure to account for the length of the post that will butt against the face of***

the end or header joist for fastening purposes plus the full post height above the deck platform. Use a reciprocating saw to cut a 1½-in.-deep notch along the face of one end of each post. The notch dimensions should match the length of the stair riser plus the thickness of the decking. Cut and notch the posts for the bottom of the staircase in the same fashion as the top two posts, but add an extra foot to the overall height of the bottom post or posts so they can be trimmed to the correct height once the layout is established. For the lag screws, drill two 1-in.-dia. × ½-in. deep counterbore holes with ⅜-in. pilot holes on the outside face of the notched areas **(See FIGURE A).**

2 Attach the top and bottom notched posts to the deck and stringers with ⅜ × 3-in. galvanized lag screws and washers, checking the posts with a carpenter's level to ensure that they're plumb **(See FIGURE B).** Be sure

FIGURE C: Tack the top rail into position on the inside faces of the stair posts and mark the cutoff height for trimming the bottom posts. The angle of the rail should be the same as the angle created by the noses of the stair treads.

FIGURE D: Use a reciprocating saw to trim the bottom posts to height, cutting along the line established by dry-fitting the top rail.

FIGURE E: Cut the ends of the top rails along the angled cutting lines so the rails will fit between the inside faces of the posts.

to keep the different post lengths in mind when attaching the four posts—longer posts get attached to the bottom of the staircase.

3 Position a top-rail board along the inside faces of the posts and angle it downward so that the top edge of the board marks the code-required height for the stair railing at both posts. Check this height at both post locations to make sure the distance to the treads is equal (be sure to measure from comparable points on the posts), then temporarily tack the board in place. Draw a trimming line along the top of the top rail where it intersects the bottom post **(See FIGURE C).** Also mark the angles on the top rails where they cross the inside faces of the posts—the ends of the top rails will be trimmed so the rail can fit between the posts. Remove the top rails.

FIGURE F: Screw the top rails into place with 3-in. galvanized deck screws. Set a baluster into place against the outside face of the top rail and check it for plumb with a carpenter's level. Mark where it meets the top edge of the top rail.

4 Trim off the tops of the bottom posts with a reciprocating saw, following the angled trimming line you drew in *Step 3* (**See FIGURE D**).

5 Cut the 2 × 4 top rails to length along the angled cutting lines, using a power miter saw or circular saw (**See FIGURE E**).

6 Attach the top rails between the top and bottom posts with 3-in. galvanized deck screws. Next, determine the distance between 2 × 2 balusters, spaced evenly between the top and bottom posts along the length of the angled top rails. Set the first baluster into position on the top rail so that it is plumb with the nearest post and long enough to reach the bottom of the stair stringer (our balusters are fastened to the outsides of the top rails and down the full width of each stringer). Mark the cutting angle at the top of the baluster (**See FIGURE F**). Since the length and angle of each baluster on the stair rail will not change, use

FIGURE G: Use the first baluster as a template for marking the rest of the balusters, and cut them to size. Use a spacer block between balusters when you attach them to the top rails.

FIGURE H: Measure the distance between the railing posts to determine the spacing for the deck rail balusters (See page 149). The spacing should remain consistent around the entire deck, without exceeding the maximum spacing requirements set by the building codes in your area.

FIGURE I: Gang-cut the deck railing balusters to size on a power miter box. Tack a spacer block to your work table and index off of it to cut all of the balusters to the same size.

FIGURE J: Cut and attach handrails to the stair and deck railings, centering the handrails across the width of the posts. Fasten the railings from below by driving screws up through the top rails and into the bottom faces of the handrails, following a diagonal line.

this first baluster as a template for marking the rest of the balusters, and gang-cut them all to size. ***Note: To add visual appeal, we bevel-cut the bottoms of each baluster to align with the bottoms of the stringer.***

7 Attach the balusters to the top rails and stringers with 2½-in galvanized deck screws, using a spacer block between each baluster to maintain equal spacing **(See FIGURE G).** Drive two screws per joint.

8 Measure, cut and notch the posts for the perimeter deck railings and attach them to the deck using the technique outlined in *Step 1.* Install 2 × 4 leveled top rails between the deck railing posts, using 2½-in. deck screws. Measure and cut balusters to fit between the deck railing posts and measure the space between posts to determine baluster spacing. Adjust as necessary so the baluster spacing remains consistent around the deck perimeter **(See FIGURE H).**

9 Gang-cut the deck railing balusters on a power miter box. Use a stop block to ensure that the balusters are uniform in length **(See FIGURE I).** Install the deck railing balusters, attaching them to the deck and the top rails with 2½-in. deck screws.

10 Cut handrails for the stair and deck railings and center them over the width of the posts (we used 2 × 6s, but check the building codes in your area for allowable handrail size). Drive 2½-in. deck screws up though the top rails and into the bottom face of the handrail to fasten the handrail in place **(See FIGURE J).** Attaching them in this fashion hides the screw heads from view for a more finished look. You can also purchase molded handrail (See page 149) at most lumberyards and home centers.

Skirting options

Hide the unsightly crawlspace beneath a deck and discourage dogs, cats, raccoons or other pests from taking refuge under the deck by installing prefabricated lattice panels. If you don't care for the look of lattice panels, you can use just about any exterior wood to create your own skirt boards. For example, short cedar fence boards would have been highly suitable as a skirting material for the deck shown here.

Start the skirting project by attaching 2 × 2 or 2 × 4 nailers across the deck posts with deck screws **(See Top photo).** Install vertical nailers along the posts to support the ends of the lattice panels where they butt against one another.

Cut the lattice panels to size using a circular saw equipped with a fine-tooth plywood blade. When trimming the lattice panels to size, clamp them with cauls on both sides of the cutting line to keep the slats from separating and try to avoid cutting through the staples that hold the lattice strips together. Attach the panels to the nailers with deck screws **(See Bottom photo).** Drill pilot holes to avoid splitting the thin lath strips.

Attach nailing strips to the deck posts to create a surface for attaching the skirting.

Use deck screws to attach the skirting material (lattice panels are used above). Using screws allows you to remove the panels easily to access the area below the deck.

Benches

Built-in benches can provide both a practical and decorative touch to deck platforms. As you plan your your deck layout, take into account how you intend to use the deck and locate the benches accordingly. While there are many bench designs, most built-in benches rest on extended posts attached directly to the deck substructure for support. It's most practical to install the bench posts before you lay the decking.

1 Mark locations for the bench posts on the joists or beams. For our project deck, we used 4 × 4 posts. Cut the posts to height (usually around 18 in. above the deck) and attach the bench posts to the beams or joists with ⅜ × 4–in. lag screws, fitted with washers **(See FIGURE A).**

2 Build the seat frames for the benches, which usually consist of 2 × 4s joined to the bench posts with 2½-in. deck screws **(See FIGURE B).** Plan the seat depth to be 14 to 16 in. deep. We angled the ends of our benches to complement the corner angles of the deck platforms.

3 Attach the seat boards. Use the same type of lumber as you'll use for for the decking and fasten the seat boards with 2½-in. deck screws **(See FIGURE C).** Ease the edges and corners of the seat boards and sand them with medium-grit sandpaper.

FIGURE A: Cut the deck posts to length and attach them to the deck joists or beams with lag bolts and washers.

FIGURE B: Build the bench seat frames from 2 × 4s. The seat frames can either be rectangular for straight runs or L-shaped for corners. the above frames angle inward at the ends to echo the angles of the deck platform.

FIGURE C: Attach the seat boards to the seat frames with 2½-in. deck screws. Overhang the ends of the seat boards and trim them to length once they're installed. For benches that wrap around an outside corner, miter the seat boards in the corner for a more finished appearance.

Finishing

Decks are usually finished with either a clear, water-resistant top-coat or with exterior wood stain. In both cases, the primary objective is to protect the wood from rot and to preserve the color. Untreated deck woods, like cedar, usually turn gray as they're exposed to the weather (although in more natural settings the gray, weathered appearance can be quite appealing).

In some cases (particularly if you've used pressure-treated lumber to build your deck), painting may be a desirable finishing option. If you choose to go this route, use oil-based paint that contains abrasive silica particles. Standard porch enamel will become extremely slippery when wet. If your local building center doesn't stock silica-blended deck paint, you can usually get them to mix some in. Make sure to stir the paint well before applying it. A paint roller with an extension pole is the best tool for painting the main surface. Use a brush for details and to get paint down in between deck boards.

Tips for finishing your deck

• Do not apply deck finish in cold weather (below 50° for most products). You'll likely end up having to remove the finish and reapply it on a warmer day.

• Use a sprayer to apply clear sealant. If you don't own a compressor-driven sprayer, you can get by with a simple mechanical sprayer like the one shown on the following page.

• Dip smaller deck parts in a trough of finishing material before installing them for thorough penetration and coverage. To make a dipping trough, simply lay a piece of heavy sheet plastic over a frame (deck posts laid next to each other on-edge can be used to make the frame).

• Select a finish that can be refreshed without the need to remove the old finish. Many penetrating clear finishes can simply be reapplied year after year to keep your deck looking fresh and new.

TIPS FOR FINISHING DECKS

Deck-finishing products include clear wood sealer-preservative (left) or an oil-based deck staining-sealer (right). Follow the manufacturer's instructions for the correct application method.

Smooth out rough areas on all exposed deck surfaces with medium-grit sandpaper. If your deck is built from cedar or treated lumber, wear a respirator to protect yourself from inhaling irritants.

Vacuum the deck before finishing. Use a wet/dry shop vacuum to remove sawdust and sandpaper grit.

Use a low-pressure sprayer to apply clear wood sealer-preservative to deck surfaces. For stain-sealers, brush or roll on the finish or use a compressor-driven paint sprayer.

Index

A

Angle brackets, 103
Angled joist hangers, 103, 133
Aquatic plants, 52-53
Ashlar *(See Cut-stone)*
Auger, gas-powered
  (See Gas-powered auger)

B

Backfilling, 29, 35, 61-64, 71
Balusters, types of, 149

Basketweave pattern,
    for decking, 104
    for pavers, 21
Batter *(See Setbacks)*
Batterboards, 108-112
Beam saddle, 124
Beam size, for decks, 99
Benches, built-in, for decks,
    94, 95, 155
Benches, posts for, 137
Bog plants, 52-53
Brickset, 60
Building codes, 15
    for deck stairs, 138-139
    for decks, 113
    for fences, 72
    for railings, 146, 149
    for water gardens, 43
Built-in benches, 147
Buried lines, 15, 114

C

Cantilevered decks, 123
Cap blocks, 63
Cattails, 52
Cedar bark chips, 37
Cedar deck boards, 102
Circular saw,
    angled cuts with, 132
    cutting notches with, 130-131
    cutting siding with, 120
    masonry blades for, 35, 60
    trimming deck boards with, 136
    trimming posts with, 82
Cobblestones, 9, 21
Codes *(See Building codes)*
Combination square, 137
Compactible gravel, 14, 19, 32-33, 56,
    59, 66-67, 71, 81, 115-116
Composite deck boards, 102
Concentric square pattern,
    for decking, 105
Concrete blocks, hollow core, in
    landscape building, 54
Concrete footings, crowning, 117
Concrete forms, tubular, 102, 113
    installing, 114-117
Concrete water gardens, 40
Concrete,
    crowning, 82
    curing, 116
    for deck posts, 102
    for setting posts, 82

purchasing, 113
ready mix, 113, 116
scheduling delivery of, 113
screeding, 116
stamping, 16-17
Construction adhesive, 63
Coping stones, 42-43, 47-48
    choosing, 48
    mortar for, 47-48
Cross-braces for gates, 86, 88
Crowning, patio subbase, 26
Cut-stone retaining wall, 56
Cypress mulch, 37

D

Deadmen, in wall construction, 56, 71
Deck boards,
    warped, 135-136
    trimming, 136
    types, 102
Deck frame,
    anatomy of, 123
    options for joinery, 124-125
Deck hardware, 102-103
Deck posts,
    cutting, 130-131
    installing, 130-133
    marking locations for, 110,112
    notching for beams, 130
    set in concrete, 114
Deck stain, 157
Deck screws, 103
Deck sealer, 157
Deckbuilding: an overview, 106-107
Decking patterns, 104-105
Decking,
    characteristics of, 134
    drivers for attaching, 135
    how to install, 135-137
    installing around posts, 137
    options for, 102
Decks,
    anatomy of, 97
    arbors for, 94, 95
    beams for, 97
    benches for, 94, 95, 155
    building codes for, 113
    cantilevered, 123
    decking for, 98, 134-137
    decking patterns, 104-105
    designing, 96 to 105
    drawing plans for, 98-99
    elevation drawing, 99
    examples of, 6-10, 92-95
    fascia for, 145
    fasteners for, 102-103
    floorplan for, 98
    framing sequence, 122
    ground-level decks, 100
    joists for, 97
    privacy screens for, 93
    finishing, 156-157
    footings for, 96, 97, 113-117
    floating, 93
    framing for, 122-133
    layout, 108-112
    ledgers for, 97, 118-121
    lumber for, 102
    multi-level, 100
    posts for, 97

railings and accessories, 146-155
retaining walls with, 94
second-story, 100
skirting for, 154
spans and spacing chart, 99
stairs for, 138-145
tools for building, 101
walk-out, 100
Decorative rock, 14
Diagonal braces, 127, 128
Dog-eared fence panel, 75
Drain pipe *(See Drain tile)*
Drain tile, 61, 56, 71
Drainage rock, 60-62, 70, 71
Drill bit extension, 67
Drill/driver types, 135
Duckweed, 52

E

Edging, 15
Edging, options for, 36-37
Elevation drawing for deck, 99
Excavating for flagstone patio, 32
Excavating for water gardens, 44-45
Excavating, general, 13
Extension cords, GFCI, 15
Extension cords, in layout, 44
Exterior wood stain, 77
Eyebolt, 85

F

Falls *(See Waterfalls)*
Fascia for deck, 145
Fasteners for decks, 102-103
Fence boards,
    attaching, 84-85
    cutting, 84-85
Fence hangers, 78, 83
Fence panels, prefabricated
    cutting, 88
    installing, 88-89
    making gates from, 88-89
    styles of, 73-75
Fence posts,
    cutting, 82
    cutting dadoes in, 76, 78
    holes for, 80-81
    setting, 80-82
    trimming, 82

Fences
    anatomy of, 76
    codes for, 72
    designing, 72-78
    examples of, 9-11, 73- 75
    framework of, 76
    laying out, 80-81
    materials for, 76
    post caps for, 76
    setback for, 76
    skirt boards for, 72
    stick-built, 80-85
    tools for building, 78
    trees and, 83-85
Fern, water, 52
Filters, water, 49
Finishes, for decks, 156-157
Finishing decks, tips for, 156
Fish, for water gardens, 52-53

Flagstone patio,
    designing, 30-32
    excavating for, 32
    installing, 32-35
    slope for, 32
    subbase for, 32-33
Flagstone, about, 30-31
Flagstones,
    arranging, 31
    buying, 31
    cutting, 33-35
    estimating, 31
    gauged, 31
    joints between, 33-34
    setting, 33-35
Flashing, 103, 119, 120
Floorplan for deck, 98
Footings, for decks, 96-97, 113-117
Fountains (See Water fountains)
Framing decks, 122-133
Frost line, 113

G

Garden hose, in layout, 24, 38
Garden ponds (See Water gardens)
Gas-powered auger, 15, 80, 115
Gate hardware,
    installing, 87
    types of, 77
Gates
    cross-braces for, 86
    examples of, 73, 74
    from prefab panels, 88-89
    hanging, 87
    how to build, 86-87
    tools for building, 78
Gauged flagstones, 31
GFCI extension cords, 15
Goldfish, 52-53
Gothic-style fence, 75
Gravel, compactible (See
    Compactible gravel)
Gravel, pea (See Pea gravel)
Ground cover, as joint filler, 34
Gussets, 125

H

Half-blocks, 61, 63
Hand saw, finishing cuts with, 141
Handrails, for deck stairs, 149, 153
Hardware, deck, 102
Herringbone pattern,
    for decking, 104
    for pavers, 21
Huckleberry picket fence, 75
Hyacinth, water, 52

I

Interlocking block retaining wall,
    cross-section of, 56
Interlocking blocks,
    cutting, 60
    installing, 58-64
    joints for, 61-62
    leveling, 60
    retaining wall, cross-section of, 56
    setting, 60-61
    types of, 57

Interlocking pavers (See Pavers)
Iris, water, 52

J

J-bolt, 114, 102, 116, 129
Jig saw, 86, 137
Joints,
    between flagstones, 33-34
    between pavers, 27
Joist hangers, 103, 125, 129, 132
Joist locations, laying out, 120-121
Joist spacing, for decks, 99
Joist spans, for decks, 99
Joist straps, 125
Joists, installing on deck, 130-132

K

Kitchen centers, for decks, 148
Kneeling board, 33
Koi, 52-53

L

Lag bolts, 102, 124
Lag screws, 102, 124
Landscape edging, 15, 32-33
    cross-section of, 37
    installing, 38-39
Landscape fabric, 15, 19, 25-26, 32-33,
    38-39, 53, 56, 61-63, 69-70, 126
Landscape spikes, 25-26, 69, 71
Landscape timber retaining wall,
    cross-sections of, 56, 71
Landscape timbers, 57
    building planting beds with, 65-70
    characteristics of, 65
    cutting, 66
    leveling, 66-67
    rough hewn, 55
    weep holes in, 69
Lap-siding walls,
    anatomy of, 119
    attaching ledger to, 119
Lattice panels, for skirting, 154
Lattice-top fence panel, 75
Layout for decks, 108-112
Ledger boards, 97, 118-121
    attaching to lap siding, 119
    attaching to masonry, 119
    attaching to stucco, 119
    locating, 119
    sizing, 118
Lettuce, water, 52
Lillies, water, 52-53
Limestone, 31, 37
Line level, 22. 111
Livestock, for water gardens, 52-53
Loose fill, 36-39
Loose-fill walkway,
    laying out, 38
    installing, 38-39
    tools for, 37
Lotus, 52
Low-pressure sprayer, 157
Lumber,
    as edging, 37
    buying, 102

M

Machine bolts, 102
Masonry blade, for circular saw,
    35, 60
Masonry saws, 27
Masonry sleeve, 119
Masonry walls,
    anatomy of, 119
    attaching ledger to, 119
Miter saw, power, 85, 151, 153
Mortar joints, curing, 34
Mortar mix, 34
    for coping stones, 47-48
    for paver joints, 29
Mortar, working with, 47
Mortared stone retaining walls, 56
Multi-level decks, 100

N

Nail gun, pneumatic (See Pneumatic
    nail gun)
Nailing strips, 154
Nails, galvanized, 102
Ninety-degree repeat pattern, for
    decking, 105

O

Off-set diamond style (pavers), 21
Organic matter, as loose fill, 36-37

P

Paint sprayer, 85, 89
Paint, exterior, 77
Patios, 16-38
    designing, 16-21
    laying out, 22-23
    slope for, 22-23, 25
Paver edging, 19
    installing, 24-26
Paver patio, anatomy of, 19
Paver patios, how to install, 22-29
Pavers,
    about, 18
    as edging, 37
    border, 28
    casting, 16-17
    cutting, 27-28
    filling joints between, 29
    laying, 26-28
    leveling, 27-28
    patterns for setting, 21
    styles of, 21
    tools for setting, 19
Pea gravel, 14, 45-46
Pier footings, precast, 96, 102, 114
Posts, for decks, 97
Pipe,
    as deck railing, 148
    as spacers, 25-26
    to stabilize fence, 84
Planter box, for deck, 147
Planting beds
    designing, 65
    examples of, 6, 8, 64
    in landscape design, 54-55
    laying out, 66
    with landscape timbers, 65-70

Plants, for water gardens, 52-53
Plate vibrator, 15, 24, 29
Platform deck, anatomy of, 97
Plumb bob, 112, 116
Plywood gussets, 125
Plywood nailers for stairs, 141
Pneumatic nail gun, 84, 85, 128
Pond liners, flexible, 40-48
    cross-section of, 43
    installing, 44-48
    sizing, 43
    subbase for, 44-46
Pond liners, rigid shell, 40-41, 43
Ponds (See Water gardens)
Portland cement, 19, 33
Post anchors, 103, 114, 129
Post caps,
    for fences, 76
    for railings, 149
Post level, 81
Post size, for decks, 99
Posthole digger, 80
Posts, trimming, 151
Preformed shell liner (See Pond liners, rigid shell)
Pressure-treated deck boards, 102
Pumps, 49-51
PVC pond liners (See Pond liners, flexible)

Q

Quartz, 36
Quartzite, 31

R

Railing-post caps, 149
Railings for decks, 146-154
    building codes for, 146, 149
    designing, 146-149
    examples of, 147-148
    installing, 150-153
Railroad ties, 65
Raised planting beds (See Planting beds)
Rebar,
    cutting, 68
    for joining timbers, 67-69, 71
    for reinforcing concrete, 114
Recirculating pumps, 51
Reference lines, in layout, 24
Reinforcing rod (See Rebar)
Retaining walls,
    cross-sections of, 56
    design and construction, 56-57, 59-64
    examples of, 7, 55, 56, 71
    in landscape design, 54
    setback of, 56
    terracing, 57, 59
Rigid-shell pond liners, 40-41, 43
River rock, 14, 36-37
Rock, decorative (See Decorative rock)
Rock, river (See River rock)
Rock, trap (See Trap rock)
Rubber pond liners (See Pond liners, flexible)
Running bond pattern, 19, 20
Running stack pattern, 21

S

Safety, 15
Sand, 14, 19
    as base for flexible liners, 44-46
    screeding, 26, 32-33
Saws, masonry, 27
Screeding concrete, 116
Screeding sand, 26, 32-33
Seat boards, for deck benches, 155
Sedimentary stones, 31, 56
Setback
    for fences, 76
    for interlocking blocks, 56, 58
    for timber retaining wall, 71
    from property lines, 15
    in retaining walls, 56
Shadowbox fence, 75, 80, 84
Site preparation, general, 13
Skirt boards, for fences, 72
Skirting, for decks, 154
Slate, 31
Slope,
    for drain tile, 61
    for flagstone patio, 32
    for paver patios, 22-23, 25
Sod kicker, 15, 23, 38, 59
Sod, laying, 29, 63-64
Spans and spacing,
  for decks (chart), 99
Split-octagon style (pavers), 21
Squaring layout lines, 110-111
Stain, exterior, 77
Stair stringer brackets, 142
Stairs, for decks, 138-145
    baluster options, 149
    box-style, 143
    building codes for, 138-139
    guidelines for, 138-139, 143
    handrails for, 149, 153
    rise-to-run ratio, 138-139
    stringers for, 139
    stringer brackets for, 142
Stick-built fences,
    definition, 79
    how to build, 80-85
Stockade fence, 75
Stocking water gardens, 52-53
Story pole, 23-24, 115
Stucco walls,
    attaching ledger to, 119
    anatomy of, 119
Subbase
    crowning, 26
    for deck posts, 115-116
    for drain tile, 61
    for fence posts, 81
    for flagstone patio, 32-33
    for flexible pond liners, 44-46
    for paver patio, 13, 19, 23-25
    for retaining walls, 59-60
Submerged plants, 53
Submersible pumps, 49
Swales, 57

T

T-strap, 103, 124, 125
Tamper, power (See Plate vibrator)
Tamping, by hand, 32, 59
Terracing, 57, 59

Timbers (See Landscape timbers)
Trap rock, 14
Tube forms (See Concrete forms, tubular)
Turnbuckles, 84-85

U

V

W

Walkways, 16-38
    designing, 16-21
    examples of, 17
    loose-fill, building, 36-39
Wall height, 54
Wall structures, 54-71
    excavating and grading for, 54, 58-60
    tools and materials for, 57
Walls, retaining (See Retaining walls)
Water filters, 49
Water fountains, 49, 51
    choosing pumps for, 51
    spray fountains, 51
    statuary fountains, 51
Water gardens,
    choosing site for, 43
    code restrictions, 43
    concrete, 40
    depth of, 43
    designing, 40-44
    estimating water volume of, 46
    examples of, 6, 7, 11, 41
    excavating for, 44-45
    livestock for, 52-53
    plants for, 52-52
    stocking, 52-53
Water, testing quality of, 53
Waterfalls,
    anatomy of, 50
    designing, 50-51
    installing, 50-51
    options for, 50-51
    pumps for, 49
Weed growth, inhibiting, 15
Weep holes, 69
Wood preservative, applying, 77
Wood sealer, 83
Worksite organization, 108

X

Y

Z

Zig-zag style pavers, 21